craft **workshop**

tin

25 step-by-step practical ideas for hand-crafted tinwork projects

Marion Elliot

photography by Peter Williams

southwater

For my parents, Arthur and Lily

This edition is published by Southwater

Southwater is an imprint of Anness Publishing Ltd
Hermes House, 88–89 Blackfriars Road, London SE1 8HA
tel. 020 7401 2077; fax 020 7633 9499
www.southwaterbooks.com; info@anness.com

© Anness Publishing Ltd 1996, 2004

UK agent: The Manning Partnership Ltd, 6 The Old Dairy,
Melcombe Road, Bath BA2 3LR; tel. 01225 478444;
fax 01225 478440; sales@manning-partnership.co.uk

UK distributor: Grantham Book Services Ltd, Isaac Newton
Way, Alma Park Industrial Estate, Grantham, Lincs NG31 9SD;
tel. 01476 541080; fax 01476 541061;
orders@gbs.tbs-ltd.co.uk

North American agent/distributor: National Book Network,
4501 Forbes Boulevard, Suite 200, Lanham, MD 20706;
tel. 301 459 3366; fax 301 429 5746; www.nbnbooks.com

Australian agent/distributor: Pan Macmillan Australia, Level
18, St Martins Tower, 31 Market St, Sydney, NSW 2000;
tel. 1300 135 113; fax 1300 135 103;
customer.service@macmillan.com.au

New Zealand agent/distributor: David Bateman Ltd, 30
Tarndale Grove, Off Bush Road, Albany, Auckland;
tel. (09) 415 7664; fax (09) 415 8892

A CIP catalogue record for this book is available from the
British Library.

Publisher: Joanna Lorenz
Senior Editor: Clare Nicholson
Designer: Roger Walker
Stylist: Georgina Rhodes
Illustrators: Vana Haggerty,
Madeleine David and Lucinda Ganderton

Previously published as *New Crafts: Tinwork*

10 9 8 7 6 5 4 3 2 1

NOTE
Working with tin is great fun and can fill many rewarding
hours. For safety, protective clothing should be worn when
cutting tin, and in addition a mask and goggles should be
worn when soldering or cutting MDF. Sharp edges should
always be filed smooth. The Publishers cannot accept any
responsibility for any injury incurred in the making of
these projects.

CONTENTS

INTRODUCTION

TINWARE, ONCE SEEN AS A QUAINT, OUTMODED CRAFT FORM, HAS RECENTLY ENJOYED A HUGE REVIVAL OF INTEREST. THE MARRIAGE OF SIMPLE, QUIET ELEGANCE TO SOLID UTILITY SEEMS ESPECIALLY APPEALING IN AN AGE DOMINATED BY THROWAWAY MATERIALS AND HIGH-TECH GADGETS. PUNCHED TIN KITCHENWARE IS ESPECIALLY POPULAR, EVOKING AS IT DOES AN ATMOSPHERE OF SIMPLE, HONEST LIVING IN A QUIETER AGE.

TIN REALLY IS AN EVERYDAY MATERIAL AND CAN BE OBTAINED QUITE READILY. THIS BOOK WILL SHOW YOU HOW TO PREPARE AND USE DIFFERENT FORMS OF TIN, FROM CANS TO SHEET METAL, TO MAKE YOUR OWN CREATIONS. EACH PROJECT IS EXPLAINED USING STEP-BY-STEP INSTRUCTIONS, AND THE BASIC TECHNIQUES AND MATERIALS ARE DISCUSSED IN DETAIL. THE GALLERY FEATURES INSPIRATIONAL WORK MADE BY ARTISTS AND CRAFTSPEOPLE USING TIN FROM VARIOUS SOURCES.

These beautifully simple items of tinware are made from galvanized tin. Each piece is made in a Greek workshop according to centuries-old traditional designs. The pieces may be left plain or embellished with a painted design.

HISTORY OF TIN

TIN HAS BEEN A POPULAR AND WIDELY USED METAL FOR MANY CENTURIES. AS LONG AGO AS 200 BC THE ROMANS WERE MINING THE TIN-RICH LANDS AROUND CORNWALL, ENGLAND. EVEN UP TO THE MID-EIGHTEENTH CENTURY, ENGLISH TIN PLATE PRODUCTION WAS A MAJOR INDUSTRY AND AN IMPORTANT INFLUENCE ON THE WORLDWIDE DEVELOPMENT OF TINWARE. AS PRODUCTION IN VARIOUS COUNTRIES DEVELOPED, SO DIFFERENT FORMS OF TINWARE RESULTED, INCLUDING PUNCHED DESIGNS AND JAPANNED WARE OR TOLEWARE. THE MOST RECENT REVIVAL IN INTEREST IN TINWARE HAS PAVED THE WAY FOR AN UPSURGE IN DESIGNS USING RECYCLED TIN.

In the early stages of the development of tinware, Cornwall had a flourishing trade, exporting tin throughout Europe and the East. The Romans recognized the value of alloying tin with copper and experimented with the process to produce bronze in a controlled way. As well as making bronze vessels, the Romans also produced finely wrought tin artefacts.

Used both in its pure form and as an alloy, tin was also added to glazes. The Assyrians had discovered a way of rendering glaze opaque by the addition of tin oxide, possibly as early as 1000 BC. The knowledge of this process spread to Europe and by the fourteenth century AD, there was a tin glaze industry in Spain and Italy that spread to Holland, Germany and England and resulted in the production of faience ware and majolica pottery. Tin oxide produced a white glaze that covered the body colour of earthenware clay completely, leaving a bright white canvas on which to paint metal oxides, such as manganese, copper and cobalt. When fired, the oxides fused with the tin glaze to produce wonderfully bright enamel-like colours. Tin was also exported further afield to the Far East, where it was put to use in the production of pewter and also as a currency.

Because it resisted tarnishing so well, tin was commonly used to plate other metals. The tin-plating process originated in Germany, but the vast majority of tin plate was produced in England, owing to the ready availability of the raw material. By the mid-eighteenth century, English tin plate production was a major industry, exporting principally to the USA.

American and English domestic tinware production flourished and popular tinware took two main forms. There were plain domestic wares such as candle holders, sconces, sieves, boxes, food containers and trays made of unpainted metal. They were left either completely unadorned or decorated by means of punching and piercing. Punching the tin with a nail or punch left indentations and holes in the metal that could be purely decorative, or functional too. For example, items such as the classic of American tinware, the Paul Revere lantern, with its distinctive conical roof, were heavily punched with perforations that were gloriously decorative and also practical. They allowed heat and

Above: These beautiful, brightly printed toys were made in India, where millions of people are involved in the collection of scrap tin and its working into new objects. The toys are made in small workshops and commercially manufactured. The decoration may be printed on the back of recycled tin sheet or the tin may be left plain.

Left: These candle lanterns are contemporary versions of traditional designs. They come from Morocco, where different regions produce their own versions of the lantern. The lanterns are made of tin plate which has been stamped and punched for decoration.

Below: These cookie cutters are made to a traditional design by Marlene Mozsak, a professional tinsmith of New York. The motifs, a heart and a cat, are commonly found in folk art. The surface of the cutters, which are made from tin plate, is distressed to give them a dark patina.

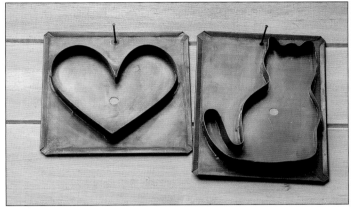

light to escape through the perforations in the tin, projecting lacy shadows on surrounding walls. Other famous examples of punched tinware were the tin panel pie safes and food cupboards that are now almost a cliché of traditional country furniture. The punched tin cabinets were not only an attractive and homely focal point but they also kept food adequately ventilated while protecting it from flies and other pests.

While punched tinware was European in origin and was produced widely in Europe, the Pennsylvania Dutch settlers of America raised tin punching to an art form, so fond were they of ornament. They decorated all sorts of domestic tinware with a dazzling array of motifs such as hearts, stars and flowers, and their designs were often of religious significance. Their tinware was in stark contrast to that of the Shaker

community, who used tin objects of great simplicity and elegance, which were beautifully designed and very functional.

The other main form of tinware was painted and was known as "japanned ware" or toleware. This was tin decorated in imitation of Japanese lacquerware, with stencils and paints. The most popular forms of toleware included trays, boxes and caddies. The tin was painted a dark colour, usually black, then decorated with a stencilled and handpainted design, such as flowers or a basket of fruit. Sometimes the background was enhanced with a fine layer of bronze powder.

During the nineteenth century, various inventions appeared that helped to commercialize the production of tinware. These included a rolling machine that could mechanically turn over and wire the edges of tinware to make it safe, and a steam

hammer that could stamp out simple forms much more quickly than could be done by hand. The revolution in the tinware industry led to a gradual decline in the production of handmade pieces in Europe and the USA, and tin was itself eventually superseded by more modern materials, such as aluminium. It is now used mainly in the canning industry to plate food containers.

However, many wonderful tin artefacts, especially those made from recycled materials, are still being produced today in places such as India and Mexico, and there has been a huge revival of interest in the tinware of such groups as the Shakers and the Pennsylvania Dutch. Original pieces are much in demand, and the craft of punching and recycling tinware has been revived by designers, craftspeople and interior designers who recognize the medium's innate charm and versatility.

GALLERY

RECYCLED TIN IS A POPULAR CHOICE FOR TINWORKERS. FOOD CANS, BOXES AND OTHER FOUND OBJECTS COST NOTHING AND MAKE IDEAL BASES FOR DECORATIVE PROJECTS, AS THEIR SHAPES CAN BECOME AN INTEGRAL PART OF THE DESIGN. THE DESIGNERS FEATURED HERE HAVE TRANSFORMED OTHERWISE THROWAWAY OBJECTS INTO ARTEFACTS WHICH WE HOPE WILL INSPIRE YOU TO DEVELOP YOUR OWN DESIGNS.

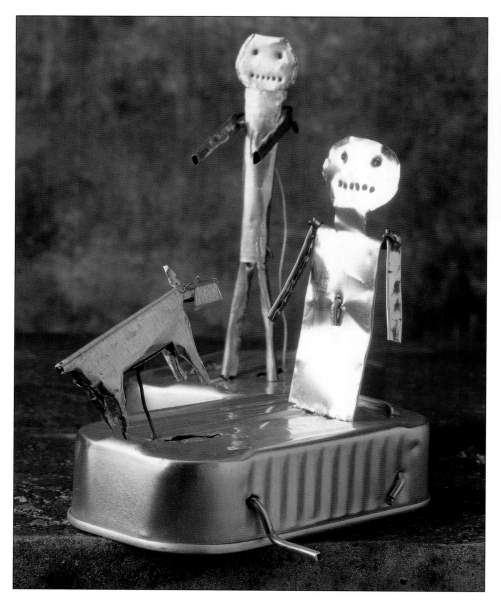

Left: TIN MAN
Plain and painted tin is Adrian's preferred medium and he uses it to make large and small objects such as these two automata. The dog and figure are mounted on a sardine tin, and when operated by a simple crank mechanism, the figure's arms move and the dog appears to jump up and down.
ADRIAN TAYLOR

Above: FIERCE ANIMALS
Lucy Casson trained as a textile designer but has worked solely in tin since 1982. This example, Fierce Animals, is typical of the animated and expressive quality of her sculptural pieces. It is constructed from recycled tin plate, which Lucy purchases from a scrap merchant, and an enamel washing bowl. The sections are joined using pop rivets and solder. Lucy does not paint her work but uses the colour already present on the surface of the tin as an integral part of the decoration.
LUCY CASSON

Above: SIN EATER, LANTERN AND COLLECTION BOX
Julia initially trained as an illustrator but has worked with non-precious metals since attending a jewellery-making course and has been recycling tin cans and boxes for several years. Her Sin Eater, made from tin cans and found objects, is inspired by the fictional account of a mysterious figure who eats the sins of the newly deceased, thus saving them. The lantern was inspired by temples and shrines seen during an Indian journey, and the hand is a collection box that belongs to another tin shrine, not shown.
JULIA FOSTER

Right: SARDINE TIN CHEST OF DRAWERS
Sardine tins, usually so carelessly disposed of, make perfect containers for paper clips, stamps and other small items of everyday life. These small tins are often beautifully decorated, for example with fishing scenes, and Michael feels that it is only sensible to give such lovely objects the second life that they so rightly deserve. He uses the tins as they are, rather than recycling them into different objects. The only modification to the tins in this chest is the addition of a wing nut to the end of each to make a handle.
MICHAEL MARRIOTT

Left: BODICE
Joanne trained as a jeweller and started working with drinks cans because she was attracted to the bright colours. She makes jewellery and one-off pieces of body sculpture, such as this shimmering evening top, which is constructed from small pieces of beer and cider cans. The edges of each small section are turned over and drilled, then linked with nickel jump rings to create a material resembling chain mail that tinkles gently as it moves.
JOANNE TINKER

Above: HAT AND NECKLACE
Val trained as a jewellery maker specializing in semi-precious metals and has enthusiastically recycled beer cans for the past ten years. She rolls the aluminium into beads to create pieces like the necklace and also forms the thin metal into amazing shapes like the hat, which is further adorned with buttons cut from iridescent compact discs. She heats the metal before using it to make it more pliable and to tone down the printed colour. She has arrived at all her techniques through constant experimentation, and has developed a range of tools to work the beer cans.
VAL HUNT

Left: COWBOY MIRROR AND SUNFLOWER MIRROR

These two mirror frames are constructed from pine and decorated with tin cut-outs recycled from old cashew nut tins. The basic shapes are cut out, filed smooth then decorated with enamel paints in bright colours. The cowboy frame is further embellished with metal studs, which are randomly hammered in to create an interesting rhinestone effect.

MARION ELLIOT

Above: THE PEACEABLE KINGDOM

This wall decoration is recycled from an old olive oil drum found outside a restaurant and is decorated using enamel paints and flowers cut from small scraps of tin. The subject matter – the peaceful co-existence of all creatures – appears frequently in folk art. Marion based her version on an allegorical painting of the eighteenth century.

MARION ELLIOT

Opposite: BERLIN
Andy Hazell is best known as a maker of automata, but this piece, Berlin, is static. The piece is a recollection of the city, a 180° condensed sweep of all the most striking features of the place. Andy used recycled biscuit tins, car body filler tins and aerosol cans, which are soldered together using electrical solder.
ANDY HAZELL

Above: FILM PROJECTOR
This beautifully crafted film projector was brought back from India by the collector Tony Hayward. It was made by a night watchman and found in a toyshop in Mysore. Made from recycled tin and wood, the projector is wired to take a 40-watt bulb. The film is fed through the machine by turning the small handle at the side.
TONY HAYWARD COLLECTION

Right: NARCISSUS SCONCE
Nick Shinnie's sconce is made from thin steel plate that has been scored with decorative cuts and polished to a soft hue. A mirror mounted in the back of the sconce reflects and intensifies the light of the candle. Nick also makes punched steel panels for wooden cabinets and dressers.
NICK SHINNIE

MATERIALS

To complete the projects in this book, you can obtain many of the materials from hardware shops and craft suppliers. For the tin plate, metal foils and sheet metals, you will need to visit a metal supplier or specialist hardware shop, or if you wish to opt for recycled materials, a metal merchant or scrap yard. Sheet metal, whether cut or uncut, is extremely sharp and should only be handled when protective leather gloves and a work shirt are worn.

Metal foils are thin sheet metals that usually come on rolls in 15 cm (6 in) and 30 cm (12 in) wide strips. Metal foil is so thin that it can be cut with a pair of household scissors. A variety of metal foils is available, including brass, aluminium and copper. The thinness of the foil makes it very soft and it is easy to draw designs into the surface.

Tin plate is generally used in place of pure tin sheet, which is prohibitively expensive. Tin plate is mild sheet steel that has been coated with tin. The tin plating is very bright and will not tarnish in the open air or in humid conditions. Sheet metals come in different thicknesses, or gauges. The higher the gauge, the thinner the metal.

There are several different gauge systems in use and they vary slightly; the Brown and Sharpe gauge in the USA and the Birmingham gauge in the UK are used to measure sheet metal. At 30 gauge (approximately 0.01 in), tin plate can be cut by hand with tin snips and shears. The edges can then be filed and hammered over before the surface of the metal is marked with a hammer and punch for decoration.

Thin zinc sheet has a dull matt surface and is fairly soft and easy to cut. It is readily available from hardware stores.

Biscuit boxes are a good source of tin. Some tins have a plastic sheen to them and so they should be scrubbed with wire wool, if you intend to solder them.

Silicon carbide paper (wet and dry paper) is very abrasive and comes in varying grades of coarseness. Fine-grade paper, when dampened, is useful for finishing off filed edges

to make them smooth. During sanding, the item should be clamped in a bench vice and the paper wrapped around a small wooden block.

Fine wire is used to join pieces of metal together and as decoration.

Paint stripper can be used to remove the paint from tin cans and boxes.

White spirit is useful for removing excess flux after soldering.

Enamel paints are dense, opaque paints that are used to paint metal.

Glass and metal paints are translucent and allow the metal to show through the coat of paint. The paint should be applied sparingly, as otherwise it can be difficult to create a smooth coat.

Wood glue is very strong PVA glue. It is white but becomes clear once it has dried.

Epoxy resin glue comes in two parts. Only mix up as much glue as you need at one time as it dries very quickly and is wasted otherwise. Once the glue has set firm, which takes about 24 hours, the join is extremely strong.

Wire wool can be used to remove the brightness from tin plate to leave a soft, brushed surface. It is also useful for cleaning the surface of metal before soldering.

Panel pins are short nails. They should be hammered in using a tack hammer.

S-joiners and jump rings are used to join sections of an object together and to attach lengths of chain. They are very strong, and pliers are used to open and close the links.

Solder is an alloy, or mixture, of metals. Solder is used to join two pieces of metal together by providing a filler of liquid metal between the surfaces. It is most important to

use a solder that has a lower melting point than the metals to be joined to avoid damaging or melting the metal. A low-melting-point solder should always be used when soldering tin, so ensure that you follow the manufacturer's instructions closely.

A flux is used during soldering to make the area to be soldered chemically clean. As the flux is heated, it runs along the metal preparing the surface so that the solder may flow smoothly and adhere properly. Some fluxes leave a corrosive residue behind which must be removed after soldering.

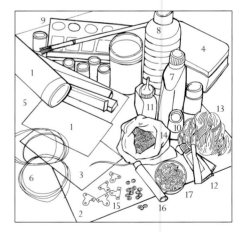

KEY

1 Metal foil	**10** Glass and metal paints
2 Tin plate	**11** Wood glue
3 Thin zinc sheet	**12** Epoxy resin glue
4 Biscuit box	**13** Wire wool
5 Silicon carbide paper	**14** Panel pins
6 Fine wire	**15** S-joiners, jump
7 Paint stripper	rings and brackets
8 White spirit	**16** Solder
9 Enamel paints	**17** A flux

EQUIPMENT

A FAIRLY BASIC SELECTION OF TOOLS IS NEEDED TO MAKE THE PROJECTS IN THIS BOOK, AND MOST OF THEM YOU MAY ALREADY HAVE. THE MORE SPECIALIZED ITEMS SUCH AS PUNCHES, SNIPS AND SHEARS ARE READILY AVAILABLE FROM GOOD HARDWARE STORES. IT IS IMPORTANT TO HAVE GOOD PROTECTIVE CLOTHING, SUCH AS GLOVES, A WORK SHIRT AND GOGGLES, FOR THE PROJECTS USING HEAVIER TIN.

Tin shears are very strong scissors for cutting sheet metal. Shears come with straight blades to cut a straight line, or blades curved to the left or right to cut circles and curves. There are also universal shears which cut straight lines and wide curves. If possible, buy a pair of shears with a spring mechanism, as this makes it much easier to open and close the blades.

Tin snips are a smaller version of tin shears and are good for cutting small shapes from a section of tin. Again, try to find a pair that has a spring mechanism.

A hide mallet is made from a roll of leather. It has a much softer head than an ordinary metal hammer and so will not make ugly marks in the tin.

A bench vice is very useful for clamping small metal shapes during filing and sanding, and when hammering over metal edges.

A wooden block with 90° edges and another with a 45° edge are used when turning over the sides of a piece of tin.

A sheet of 20 mm (¾ in) chipboard is used as a work surface when punching tin and embossing foil, as it has slightly more give than wood.

Round-nosed pliers have round jaws that are good for making small circles of wire. Flat-nosed pliers grip very well and are useful for turning over the edges of tin. You can also use snipe-nosed pliers that have long jaws that are useful for reaching inside narrow shapes and when working with fiddly things such as jump rings.

A pair of compasses is useful for drawing out circles on tin.

A tin opener is used for taking the tops off tin cans.

Hammers come in a variety of sizes. A medium-sized ball head hammer is used with nails or a punch to make a pattern in tin. A tack hammer is used to knock panel pins into wood or medium-density fibreboard (MDF). A heavier hammer is used with a chisel to make decorative holes in a sheet of metal.

A small hand file is used to remove any burrs of metal from the tin after a shape has been cut out. Files come in varying grades of coarseness, from rough to super smooth.

A centre punch is traditionally used to mark the centre of a hole in a sheet of metal before it is drilled. It can be used to punch a decorative pattern into tin.

A small chisel can be used to make a decorative pattern in tin. When tapped with a ball head hammer, it will leave a short, straight mark in the surface of the metal.

A bradawl is used to make holes.

Nails in various sizes can be used to make a pattern in a piece of tin.

A soldering iron is used to heat the solder that joins two pieces of metal together. Soldering irons may be electric or gas powered. Soldering irons have a tip known as a bit, which is kept at a constant temperature, during use. The bit should be cleaned with a file before use, then heated and dipped into flux. A little solder should be applied and allowed to coat the tip. This is called tinning the bit and will stop the solder sticking to the iron during soldering.

Protective leather gloves and a long-sleeved work shirt should always be worn when handling unfinished metal or sheet metal and during soldering.

A variety of fireproof soldering mats is readily available and may be purchased from good hardware stores and metal supply shops.

A protective mask and goggles should be worn during soldering, as the process produces fumes. Protective goggles should be worn when carrying out work that might produce small shards of metal.

Wooden pegs or masking tape can be used to hold two sections of metal together while they are soldered.

A drill is needed to make holes for screws in many of the projects. Use a metal drill bit.

Pliers are useful for holding tin when you are cutting it and also for turning over edges.

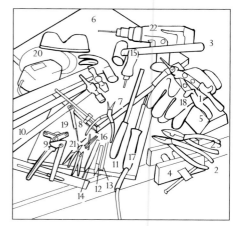

KEY
1 Tin shears	**12** Centre punch
2 Tin snips	**13** Chisel
3 Hide mallet	**14** Hand file
4 Bench vice	**15** Bradawl
5 45° Block of wood	**16** Nails
6 Chipboard	**17** Soldering iron
7 Round-nosed pliers	**18** Leather gloves
8 Pair of compasses	**19** Soldering mat
9 Tin opener	**20** Mask and goggles
10 Hammers	**21** Clothes pegs
11 Hacksaw blade	**22** Drill
	23 Pliers

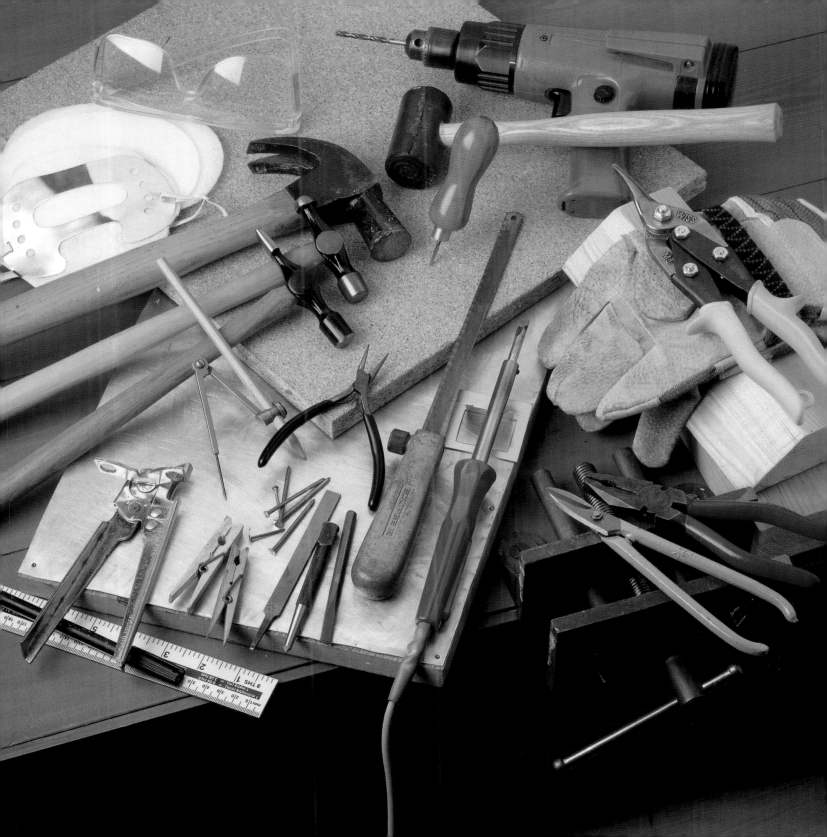

BASIC TECHNIQUES

ALTHOUGH AN EXPERT TINSMITH IS A HIGHLY SKILLED CRAFTSPERSON, THERE ARE ONLY A FEW BASIC TECHNIQUES THAT THE NOVICE TINWORKER NEEDS TO LEARN WHEN EMBARKING ON SIMPLE PROJECTS. THESE ARE CUTTING TIN, FINISHING THE EDGES, SOLDERING AND DECORATING WITH PUNCHED DESIGNS. THE MOST IMPORTANT TECHNIQUES ARE THOSE THAT RELATE TO SAFETY AND IT IS ESSENTIAL THAT THESE ARE OBSERVED EVERY TIME TO AVOID ACCIDENTS. READ THROUGH THESE TECHNIQUES BEFORE STARTING THE PROJECTS.

SAFETY ADVICE

- A heavy work shirt and protective leather gloves should always be worn when handling either cut metal pieces or uncut sheet metal.

- Tin shears and snips are very powerful, being strong enough to cut through fairly heavy metal, and very sharp. They should be handled with respect and, like all other tools, should always be kept in a safe place well away from children during and after use.

- A protective face mask and goggles should always be worn during soldering as the hot metal, solder and flux give off fumes. Work should always be carried out on a soldering mat and the iron placed on a metal rest when not in use.

- Soldering should always be carried out in a well-ventilated area and frequent breaks should be taken when working. Don't lean too near your work during soldering to avoid close contact with fumes.

- Always wear protective gloves when soldering, as the soldering iron and metal tend to get very hot.

- Always clean up as you work. Collect any small shards of tin together as you cut and make sure you don't leave any on the floor where people and animals might walk on them.

CUTTING TIN

With proper protective clothing and tin shears or snips, it is surprisingly easy to cut through thin sheets of tin plate, tin cans and so on. Tin shears are very powerful, and cutting tin with them is rather like cutting a sheet of paper. It is important to get used to cutting smoothly to avoid making jagged edges, so practise first on scraps of tin to get a feel for cutting metal. Cutting tin produces small shards of metal which are razor-sharp, so it is essential to collect scraps as you cut and keep them together until you can dispose of them safely.

Cutting a Section from a Sheet

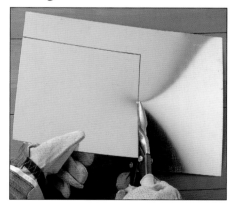

1 To cut a section of tin from a large sheet, it is necessary to use tin shears. It is important to avoid creating a jagged edge when cutting, for safety reasons, and the secret of achieving a smooth cut is never to close the blades of the shears completely. Instead, make a cut almost the length of the

blades each time, open the shears, then gently guide the metal back into the blades and continue. Keep the blades of the shears in the cut, without removing them until the line of the cutting is complete. If you are cutting a straight-sided shape, don't try to turn the shears around once you have reached a corner. Remove the shears and cut across to the corner from the edge of the sheet of metal.

Cutting a Small Shape from a Section of Tin

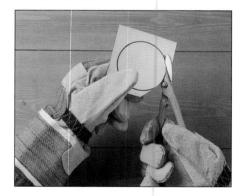

1 If you are cutting a small shape from a section of tin, it is better to use a pair of tin snips than shears. They are easier to manipulate and control, especially if you are cutting an intricate shape. Again, don't attempt to turn the snips around in the metal: cut as much as you can, then remove the snips and turn the metal so that you can follow the cutting line more easily.

Cutting a Panel of Metal from an Oil Drum

Oil drums are an excellent source of large areas of smooth, flat metal. It is very common to find discarded oil drums outside wholesale food importers, restaurants and cafés and they can be recycled very easily. As many of the drums are printed with bright, highly decorative designs, it is possible to use both sides of the metal.

1 To cut a panel from an oil drum, first remove the top. Make a cut in the side of the drum using a hacksaw blade. Open the sides of the cut slightly, then insert the blades of a pair of tin shears into the space and cut around the drum, removing the top. The metal found in oil drums is very often quite thin and springy, and so care must be taken when cutting out panels from a drum. Protect your eyes with goggles for extra safety.

2 Once you have removed the top of the drum, carefully cut down one side to within 2 cm (¾ in) of the base using tin shears. Gently snip around the base of the drum, carefully pushing back the panel as it is freed from the base. Once you have removed the panel completely, it may be used in the same way as a sheet of tin plate. Mop up any oil residue on the surface of the tin using tissue paper.

FINISHING THE EDGES

All tin items should be considered unfinished and unsuitable for use until all the edges have been smoothed or turned over. This should be done immediately to avoid accidents. Long, straight edges may be folded back and flattened with the aid of a hammer and wooden blocks with measured 90° and 45° edges. Irregularly shaped items may be finished with a hand file and wet and dry paper for complete smoothness. Items such as tin cans should always be filed smooth around the rims before use to remove any jagged edges.

Filing Cut Metal

1 Obviously, the raw, cut edges of a piece of tin plate are very sharp indeed, and should be immediately smoothed or finished in some way to prevent them causing harm to yourself or anyone else. Small shapes should be smoothed with a hand file while firmly clamped in a bench vice. The file should be moved forwards at a right angle to the metal in one light stroke, then lifted and returned. This will remove most of the rough edges.

Finishing Rough Edges with Wet and Dry Paper

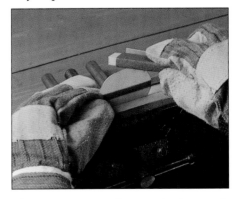

1 To make a cut edge completely smooth after filing, it should be finished with fine-grade silicon carbide paper, also known as wet and dry paper. This is dampened and wrapped around a small wooden block. Sanding with wet and dry paper will remove any remaining rough edges and leave the metal smooth to the touch.

Turning Over Cut Edges

The cut edges of straight-sided pieces of tin plate should be turned over immediately after cutting to avoid accidents. Mechanically made baking tins and boxes have their edges bent over to an angle of 45° by a folding machine. The edges are then pressed flat and made safe. It is simple to replicate this process at home using two blocks of wood.

1 First, a thick block of wood with an accurately measured 90° edge is clamped firmly in a bench vice. A border, say 1 cm (½ in) wide, is drawn around the cut edges of the tin plate. The piece of tin is placed on the block with the border line lying along the edge of the wooden block. The edge of the tin is then struck smartly with a hide hammer which moulds the metal around the edge of the wooden block to an angle of 90°.

2 Once the edge of the metal has been folded halfway over, the piece of tin is turned over and a block of wood with a 45° edge is placed inside the fold. The wooden block is kept firmly in position with one hand and the folded edge is hammered down upon it using a hide hammer. Once the metal has been folded over to this angle, the block is removed, and the edge is then hammered completely flat using a hide hammer. Each side of the piece of tin is folded in turn and, once all the edges have been hammered flat, the corners should be filed to smooth any sharp edges. All straight edges should be finished in this way to avoid accidents, even if the panel is to be set into a recess, for example in the case of a punched-panel cabinet.

DECORATING TIN

Tin may be decorated in a variety of ways. Punching, when a pattern of indentations is beaten into the surface of the metal, is one of the most common methods. A centre punch or nail, plus a ball hammer, are used to produce the knobbly patterns, either on the front or back of the tin. Small chisels and metal stamps are also used. Opaque and translucent enamel paints are suitable for decorating tin plate and some other metals. Any grease or dirt should be removed first before painting. Very thin metal foils, such as aluminium foil, are so soft that a design may be drawn on to the surface, to leave a raised or "embossed" pattern.

Getting the Design Right

1 Nails or punches can be used to make indentations and holes in tin. If you want to emboss a sophisticated pattern, then it is a good idea to draw the design out on a sheet of graph paper first and punch through the paper into the tin following the lines. The paper should be taped to the tin, and the tin attached to a piece of chipboard using panel pins to keep it steady as you punch.

Punching Tin from the Front

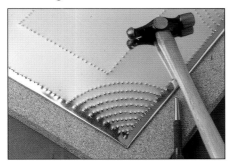

1 A design may be punched into either the front or the back of a piece of tin. If it is punched from the front, the resulting pattern will be indented. If it is punched from the back, the pattern will be raised. If an area of tin is punched from the front, and the indentations are made very close together, the punched area recedes and the unpunched area becomes slightly raised. This is a form of "chasing", where decorative patterns are punched into metal from the front and stand out in low relief.

Punching Tin from the Back

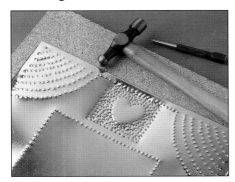

1 Punching a pattern into a piece of tin from the back leaves a very pleasing knobbly effect on the surface of the tin. Pattern can be applied with nails of different sizes or punches to make a dotty texture. Short lines can be made by using a small chisel. It is also possible to buy decorative punches that have designs engraved into the tip.

Embossing Aluminium Foil

1 Aluminium foil is very soft, thin metal rather like kitchen foil. It can be easily cut with household scissors and bent or folded as desired, so it is especially useful for cladding frames, books, boxes and other small items. Its softness makes it very easy to emboss and this is done by drawing on to the back of the foil using a ballpoint pen, which leaves a raised surface on the other side. It is best to use an empty ballpoint pen as it makes the process cleaner.

SOLDERING

Sections of metal may be joined together by soldering. It is essential that both surfaces to be joined are clean before they are soldered. Rubbing both areas with wire wool will help to remove any dirt and grease. All soldering should be done on a soldering mat, wearing protective gloves, mask and goggles, and the soldering iron should be placed on a metal stand when not in use.

1 The two sections to be joined are placed together. They may be held in place with wooden pegs or masking tape if required. Before the joint is soldered, it is smeared with flux. This is essential, as when the metal is heated, an oxide forms on the surface which may inhibit the adhesion of the solder. The flux prevents the oxide from forming on the metal.

2 The hot soldering iron heats the metal which causes the flux to melt. A small amount of solder is picked up on the end of the iron and starts to melt. The iron is drawn down the joint and the solder flows with it, displacing the flux. The solder then cools and solidifies, joining the two pieces of metal together.

EMBOSSED GREETINGS CARDS

IT IS CURRENTLY VERY FASHIONABLE TO MAKE GREETINGS CARDS WITH ALUMINIUM FOIL MOTIFS. THE FOIL IS VERY SOFT AND EASY TO CUT WITH SCISSORS. DESIGNS CAN BE DRAWN INTO THE BACK OF THE FOIL TO MAKE A RAISED, EMBOSSED SURFACE THAT IS VERY ATTRACTIVE AND RESEMBLES STAMPED TIN. ANTIQUE ENGRAVINGS ARE A GOOD SOURCE OF INSPIRATION WHEN DECIDING ON MOTIFS, AND BOOKS CONTAINING COLLECTIONS OF OLD DESIGNS CAN BE BOUGHT. THE FOIL IS RELATIVELY CHEAP TO BUY AND CAN BE OBTAINED FROM HOBBY SHOPS AND SCULPTOR'S SUPPLIERS IN VARIOUS THICKNESSES; 36 GAUGE (0.005 IN) IS EASY TO USE, MAKING IT SUITABLE FOR NEW TINWORKERS.

1 Trace the card motifs from the templates on page 91. Tape the tracing to a piece of aluminium foil and place it on top of a piece of thin card. Carefully draw over the lines of the motif with a ballpoint pen to transfer it to the foil.

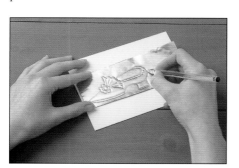

2 Remove the tracing paper from the foil and redraw over the lines of the motif to make the embossing deeper. Add detail to the design at this stage.

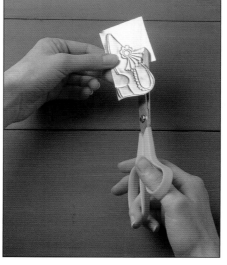

3 Turn the sheet of foil over and cut around the motif, leaving a narrow margin around the outline of the design.

4 Cut a piece of thick coloured paper and fold it in half to make a greetings card. Spread a little glue over the back of the foil motif and stick it to the card, embossed side up.

MATERIALS AND EQUIPMENT YOU WILL NEED

TRACING PAPER • SOFT PENCIL • MASKING TAPE • 36 GAUGE (0.005 IN) ALUMINIUM FOIL • THIN CARD • BALLPOINT PEN • SCISSORS • THICK COLOURED PAPER • ALL-PURPOSE GLUE

CANDLE COLLARS

CANDLE COLLARS ARE A CLEVER MEANS OF MAKING CANDLES AND CANDLESTICKS LOOK EXTREMELY DECORATIVE. THEY CAN BE USED ON A FLAT SURFACE AS A SURROUND FOR SERENE CHURCH CANDLES, OR THEY CAN SIT ATOP A PLAIN CANDLESTICK FOR A TOUCH OF RESTRAINED GLAMOUR. THESE CANDLE COLLARS ARE BASED ON FLOWER AND LEAF FORMS AND ARE EMBOSSED FROM THE BACK IN IMITATION OF VEINING. THE BEADING, THOUGH SEEMINGLY INTRICATE, IS VERY SIMPLE TO ATTACH TO THE SOFT METAL FOIL USING THIN JEWELLER'S WIRE. CANDLES CAN BE A FIRE HAZARD, ESPECIALLY IF THEY ARE FREE-STANDING, AND SO THEY SHOULD NEVER BE LEFT TO BURN UNATTENDED.

1 Trace the template on page 91, enlarging it if necessary, then transfer it to thin card and cut out the shape. Tape the template to a piece of copper foil. Draw around the template using a sharp pencil to transfer the shape to the foil.

3 Place the collar face down on a sheet of thin card. Redraw over the lines of the outer and inner circles using a ballpoint pen. Press a random pattern of dots into the surface of the foil between the two rings. Draw veins on each petal.

5 To attach the beads to the collar, thread a length of fine wire through the first hole in the collar, from the back to the front, leaving a 2.5 cm (1 in) end. Bend the end back to keep the wire in place. Thread a large glass bead on to the wire, then a smaller bead. Loop the wire over the smaller bead, then back down through the large bead to the back of the collar and on to the next hole. When all the beads are attached, cut the wire leaving an end. Twist the two ends of the wire together to keep the beads in place.

2 Remove the template and cut around the outside of the collar. Pierce the centre of the collar using a bradawl. Insert the scissors through the hole and carefully cut out the centre of the collar.

4 Place the embossed collar face up on a block of wood. Carefully pierce a hole directly below the centre of each petal using a bradawl.

MATERIALS AND EQUIPMENT YOU WILL NEED

TRACING PAPER • SOFT PENCIL • THIN CARD • SCISSORS • MASKING TAPE • 40 GAUGE (0.003 IN) COPPER FOIL • SHARP PENCIL • BRADAWL • BALLPOINT PEN • WOODEN BLOCK • FINE JEWELLER'S WIRE • GLASS BEADS

PAINTED TIN BROOCHES

A GOOD WAY TO USE UP SMALL SCRAPS OF TIN IS TO MAKE BROOCHES. THESE CAN BE VERY SIMPLE IN CONSTRUCTION AND MADE SPECIAL WITH PAINTED DECORATION. ENAMEL PAINTS ARE VERY OPAQUE AND COVER PREVIOUS COATS OF PAINT BEAUTIFULLY, SO LIGHT COLOURS CAN BE PAINTED ON TOP OF DARK VERY SUCCESSFULLY. THIS AFFORDS GREAT FREEDOM OF DESIGN AND THE ONLY RULE TO OBSERVE IS THAT PLENTY OF TIME MUST BE ALLOWED FOR ONE COAT OF PAINT TO DRY BEFORE THE NEXT IS APPLIED. THIS IS ALSO TRUE WHERE DIFFERENT COLOURS ARE PAINTED CLOSE TO EACH OTHER; IT IS BEST TO LEAVE SMALL GAPS BETWEEN THE COLOURS AND FILL THEM IN WHEN THE PAINT HAS DRIED.

1 To make the brooch front, draw a circle measuring 5 cm (2 in) in diameter freehand on a piece of tin. Wearing a work shirt and protective gloves, cut out the circle using tin snips.

3 Draw the outline of the sun on to one side of the brooch using a chinagraph pencil. Paint around the outline with enamel paint, then fill in the design. Leave the brooch to dry thoroughly.

5 Seal the surface of the brooch with two coats of clear gloss polyurethane varnish to protect the paint from scratches. Leave the varnish to dry thoroughly before applying the second coat.

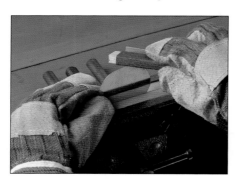

2 Clamp the circle of tin in a bench vice and file the edges. Finish off the edges with damp wet and dry paper so that they are completely smooth (see Basic Techniques).

4 Paint in the background then the sun's features on top of the first coat of paint, using a fine paintbrush and enamel paint. Leave the brooch to dry thoroughly.

6 Mix some epoxy resin glue and use it to stick a brooch fastener on to the back. Let the glue dry thoroughly before wearing the brooch.

MATERIALS AND EQUIPMENT YOU WILL NEED

SCRAP OF 30 GAUGE (0.01 IN) TIN • MARKER PEN • WORK SHIRT AND PROTECTIVE LEATHER GLOVES • TIN SNIPS • BENCH VICE • FILE • WET AND DRY PAPER • CHINAGRAPH PENCIL • ENAMEL PAINTS • FINE PAINTBRUSHES • CLEAR GLOSS POLYURETHANE VARNISH • EPOXY RESIN GLUE • BROOCH FASTENER

PUNCHED PANEL CABINET

THIS CABINET WITH ITS PUNCHED TIN PANEL IS BASED ON THOSE MADE BY THE PENNSYLVANIA DUTCH COMMUNITIES OF AMERICA, WHO PRODUCED A WIDE RANGE OF HOUSEHOLD ARTEFACTS USING TIN PLATE AND RAISED THE DECORATIVE PUNCHING PROCESS TO AN ART FORM. THEY PUNCHED INDENTATIONS AND HOLES INTO THE METAL FOR AESTHETIC REASONS AND ALSO FOR PRACTICALITY; TO ALLOW AIR TO CIRCULATE AND TO KEEP OUT PESTS IN THE CASE OF CABINETS, OR TO SHED LIGHT FROM TIN LANTERNS. TRADITIONAL PATTERNS SUCH AS HEARTS, TULIPS AND STARS LOOK WONDERFUL PICKED OUT ON THE SURFACE OF THE TIN, OR YOU COULD EXPERIMENT BY DESIGNING YOUR OWN PATTERNS. SIMPLE, UNCLUTTERED DESIGNS WORK BEST; ORNATE, COMPLICATED DESIGNS TEND TO BE A LITTLE CONFUSING TO "READ".

1 Measure the recess in the door of the cabinet. Add 2 cm (¾ in) to each of the dimensions and mark the dimensions on a sheet of tin using a marker pen. Draw a 1 cm (½ in) border around the inside of the rectangle. Measure and mark a point 2 cm (¾ in) from each corner of the outer rectangle. Draw diagonal lines from these points to the corners of the inner rectangle.

2 Wearing a work shirt and protective leather gloves, cut the panel from the sheet of tin using tin shears. Cut along the diagonal lines at the corners.

3 Firmly clamp the 90° block of wood in the bench vice. Place the panel on the wooden block with the ruled edge of the tin resting on the edge of the block. Using a hide hammer, tap along the edge of the panel to turn it over to an angle of 90°.

▶

MATERIALS AND EQUIPMENT YOU WILL NEED

SMALL WOODEN CABINET WITH A RECESS IN THE DOOR • RULER • SHEET OF 30 GAUGE (0.01 IN) TIN PLATE • MARKER PEN • WORK SHIRT AND PROTECTIVE LEATHER GLOVES • TIN SHEARS • BENCH VICE • 90° AND 45° WOODEN BLOCKS • HIDE HAMMER • FILE • GRAPH PAPER • SCISSORS • PAIR OF COMPASSES • PENCIL • MASKING TAPE • SHEET OF CHIPBOARD • PANEL PINS • TACK HAMMER • CENTRE PUNCH • BALL HAMMER • SMALL CHISEL

4 Turn the panel over. Position the 45° wooden block inside the turned edge and hammer the edge over it. Remove the block and hammer the edge completely flat. Finish the remaining three sides of the panel in the same way. Carefully file the corners of the panel to remove any sharp edges.

5 Cut a piece of graph paper the same size as the panel. Using a pair of compasses and a ruler, draw out the panel design on the paper to make a pattern.

6 Tape the paper pattern to the front of the panel. Place the panel face up on a sheet of chipboard and secure each corner to the board with a panel pin.

7 Place the centre punch on one of the lines. Tap the punch with the ball hammer to make an indentation in the tin. Move the punch about 3 mm (⅛ in) along the line and tap the punch to make the next mark. Continue punching along the lines until the design is completed.

8 Unpin the panel from the board and remove the paper pattern. Pin the panel to the board again and add extra decoration to the front of the panel using a small chisel.

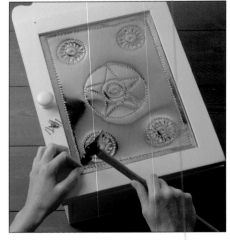

9 Unpin the panel from the board. Place the panel in the recess on the front of the cabinet and attach it to the cabinet with a panel pin at each corner.

INCENSE HOLDER

DEVOTIONAL ARTEFACTS ARE ALWAYS INSPIRATIONAL BECAUSE THEY COMBINE STURDY PRACTICALITY WITH WONDERFUL DECORATIVE DETAIL. THIS ORNATE INCENSE HOLDER IS REMINISCENT OF ECCLESIASTICAL CENSERS, WHICH ARE USED IN RELIGIOUS SERVICES AND PROCESSIONS. TWO COLOURS OF METAL FOIL ARE HEAVILY EMBOSSED AND USED TO ENCASE A HUMBLE TIN CAN. TRANSLUCENT GLASS DROPS, WHICH CAN BE PURCHASED FROM HABERDASHERS AND JEWELLERY SUPPLIERS, ARE SUSPENDED FROM A FOIL COLLAR TO GIVE A FEELING OF OPULENCE, WHILE THE TIN IS STUDDED WITH SMALL FLOWERS WITH CABOCHON CENTRES. THIS HOLDER IS DESIGNED TO BURN SMALL INCENSE CONES, WHICH SIT INSIDE THE TIN IN A METAL BOTTLE CAP. SMOULDERING INCENSE CAN BE A FIRE HAZARD AND SHOULD NOT BE LEFT TO BURN UNATTENDED.

1 Using a tin opener, remove one end of the tin can. Carefully file around the inside top edge of the tin to remove metal burrs or rough edges. To make the covering for the tin, cut a rectangle of aluminium foil as wide as the tin, and long enough to fit around it with 1 cm (½ in) to spare.

2 Using this pattern as a guide, draw out a design on to graph paper. Repeat the pattern to fit around the tin and cut it out. Tape the aluminium foil to a sheet of card. Tape the pattern over the top and draw over the lines using a ballpoint pen. Press quite hard so that the pattern will be embossed on to the foil.

3 Cut a shorter, narrower rectangle of aluminium foil to make the lower section. Draw out the decorative pattern for this section on to graph paper. Cut out the paper pattern and transfer it to the narrower strip of aluminium foil as before, using a ballpoint pen.

▶

MATERIALS AND EQUIPMENT YOU WILL NEED

TIN OPENER • SMALL TIN CAN • FILE • 36 GAUGE (0.005 IN) ALUMINIUM FOIL • SCISSORS • PENCIL • GRAPH PAPER • MASKING TAPE • THIN CARD • BALLPOINT PEN • 40 GAUGE (0.003 IN) COPPER FOIL • EPOXY RESIN GLUE • WOODEN POLE • BENCH VICE • BRADAWL • THIN METAL CHAIN • 3 CHAIN TRIANGLES • PLIERS • KEY RING • SMALL COLOURED GLASS DROPS AND STONES • CARDBOARD TUBE • METAL BOTTLE CAP

4 Draw a flower pattern on thin white card and cut it out to make a template. Draw around the template on to copper foil and cut out the shape. Cut as many flowers as you need to fit around the tin. Place the flowers on thin card and draw lines on to the petals to make a decoration.

6 Cut three 13 cm (5 in) lengths of chain. Fix a chain triangle through each hole in the top of the tin and, using pliers, attach a length of chain to each. Attach the other ends of the chains to a key ring.

8 Snip tabs along the top edge of the lower section of the aluminium foil. Wrap it around a cardboard tube and glue the edges together. Leave to dry and remove from the tube. Bend out the tabs and glue to the underside of the tin.

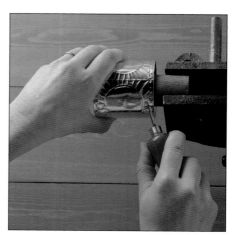

5 Glue the covering around the tin using epoxy resin glue. When the glue is dry, firmly clamp a short length of wooden pole in a bench vice. Rest the tin on the pole and make three holes at equal distances in the top edge using a bradawl. File around the edges of the holes to make them smooth.

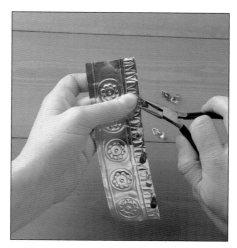

7 Make a hole every 2 cm (¾ in) along the bottom edge of the lower section of the burner using a bradawl. Attach a small glass drop to each hole.

9 Glue the copper flowers around the tin with the raised surfaces facing outwards. Glue a glass stone in the centre of each flower, alternating the colours of the stones.

10 To make a holder for the incense cone, glue a metal bottle cap to the inside centre of the tin.

PHOTOGRAPH FRAME

Because of its softness, fine-gauge aluminium foil is the perfect material for cladding frames. Coloured and clear glass nuggets combine with the subdued tones of the foil to give this frame a Celtic air, further reinforced by a design of repeating circles, a fundamental element of Celtic decorative art. Until recently, glass nuggets, a staple material of stained glass artists, were difficult to find. Now they are popular as a decorative device in their own right, especially in conjunction with floating candles, and are widely available in a variety of colours, finishes and sizes.

1 Remove the glass and backing from the frame. Measure the four sides and cut strips of foil to cover them, making the foil long enough to wrap over and under, to the back. Mould the foil strips around the frame and glue them in place.

2 Cut pieces of foil to cover the corners. Mould these to the contours of the frame and glue them in place.

3 Draw a circle on to card. Cut out the circle to make a template. Draw around the card on to the foil using a ballpoint pen. Cut out the foil circles. Draw a design on to one side of each circle. This is now the back of the circle.

4 Turn the foil circles over so that the raised side of the embossing is face up. Glue coloured glass nuggets to the centre fronts of half of the foil circles. Glue plain glass nuggets to the centres of the other half.

5 Glue the foil circles around the frame, spacing them evenly. Alternate the circles so that a coloured glass centre follows one with clear glass. When the glue is thoroughly dry, replace the glass and backing in the frame.

MATERIALS AND EQUIPMENT YOU WILL NEED

PHOTOGRAPH FRAME • RULER • 36 GAUGE (0.005 IN) ALUMINIUM FOIL • SCISSORS • EPOXY RESIN GLUE • PENCIL • THIN CARD •
BALLPOINT PEN • COLOURED AND CLEAR GLASS NUGGETS

Lantern

This tin can lantern is reminiscent of Moroccan lanterns that have similar curlicues and punched holes. A cold chisel and heavy hammer are used to cut ventilation holes out of the metal of the lantern roof. This allows heat to escape and projects dancing shadows on to walls and ceilings. The materials needed for the lantern are very humble: a large tin can, fine wire and scraps of aluminium sheet and tin plate combine wonderfully to make an attractive light source and focus in a room. Candles can be a fire hazard and should never be left to burn unattended.

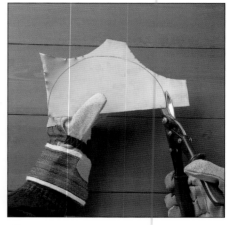

1 Using a tin opener, remove one end of the tin can. To make an aperture for the door of the lantern, mark out a rectangle on the front of the can. Wearing a work shirt and protective gloves, cut out the rectangle using tin shears.

2 Using pliers, turn over all the edges around the aperture to make the lantern safe. File away any remaining rough edges to make them safe.

3 To make the lantern lid, draw a semi-circle on a scrap of aluminium sheet. The radius of the semi-circle should be equal to the diameter of the tin can. Cut out the shape using tin shears and carefully file the edges smooth.

Materials and Equipment You Will Need

Tin opener • Large tin can • Marker pen • Work shirt and protective leather gloves • Tin shears •
Pliers • File • Thin aluminium sheet • Pair of compasses • Pencil • Sheet of chipboard • Protective goggles •
Cold chisel • Hammer • Nail or centre punch • Scrap of thin tin • Soldering mat • Flux •
Soldering iron and solder • Fine wire • Wire cutters

4 Lay the lid on a sheet of chipboard. Wearing goggles, cut ventilation holes in the lid using a cold chisel and hammer. File the sides of all the holes to remove any rough edges.

6 To make a candle holder for the inside of the lantern, cut a strip of tin. File the edges of the strip and curve it around to make a circle. Place the lantern on a soldering mat. Apply flux to the join. Wearing a protective mask and goggles, solder the holder inside the lantern.

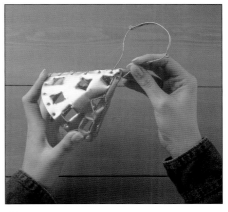

8 For the handle, cut a length of wire, then cut two shorter pieces. Make a loop in either end of the shorter pieces, then centre them on either side of the longer wire and solder in place. Curve them slightly, then thread the ends through the holes in the top of the lid and twist them into tight spirals inside to secure the handle.

5 Using a hammer and nail or centre punch, punch holes around the top edge of the lantern and around the bottom and the curved edge of the lid. File away all the rough edges around the holes.

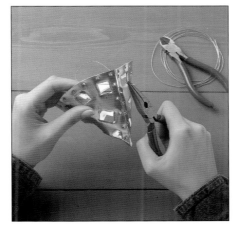

7 Gently curve the lid around to make a cone. Using a pair of pliers, thread fine wire through the holes in the lid to join the sides together.

9 Attach the lid to the lantern using fine wire. Pull the wire tight using pliers. ▶

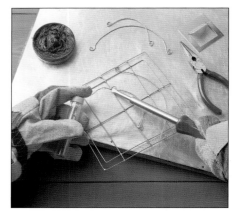

10 For the door, make a decorative rectangular frame from lengths of fine wire. The frame must be slightly taller and wider than the aperture. Lay the frame on a soldering mat and solder all the sections together. When the door is complete, gently curve it to the shape of the lantern.

12 For the latch, make a hook and a "U"-shaped catch from short lengths of wire using pliers. Solder the catch to the side of the lantern and attach the hook to the door frame.

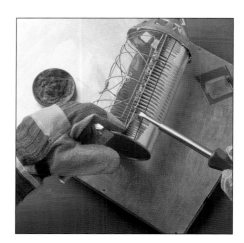

11 To make hinges for the door, use pliers to bend two short lengths of wire into "U" shapes and bend down each end of the "U" at right angles. Solder one end of each hinge to the lantern. Place the door inside the hinges so that it rests on the hinges and doesn't drop down. Solder the other end of the hinges to the lantern.

CHRISTMAS DECORATIONS

THESE TWINKLY CHRISTMAS DECORATIONS ARE INSPIRED BY EASTERN EUROPEAN ARCHITECTURE AND FOLK ART. STAMPED AND DIE-CUT ARTEFACTS WERE VERY POPULAR IN MANY EUROPEAN COUNTRIES IN THE NINETEENTH CENTURY, WHEN THERE WOULD HAVE BEEN A TINWORKER IN EVERY VILLAGE. THE DECORATIONS ARE MADE OF THIN FOIL WHICH CAN BE POLISHED WITH A SOFT CLOTH AFTER EMBOSSING TO BRIGHTEN THE METAL. THERE ARE MANY TRADITIONAL FOLK ART MOTIFS THAT COULD BE USED TO CONTINUE THE SET OF DECORATIONS, SUCH AS HEARTS, BIRDS AND FLOWERS. LOOK TO EASTERN EUROPEAN EMBROIDERY, AMERICAN FOLK ART AND COUNTRY FURNITURE FOR INSPIRATION.

1 Trace the outline from the template on page 92, enlarge if necessary, and transfer it to thin card. Cut it out to make a template. Cut a small piece of aluminium foil. Place the template on the foil and draw around the outside using a sharp pencil.

2 Using embroidery scissors, cut out the foil shape. Cut slowly and carefully to ensure that there are no rough edges around the decoration.

3 Using the picture as a guide, carefully mark the basic lines of the design on the back of the decoration using a marker pen and ruler.

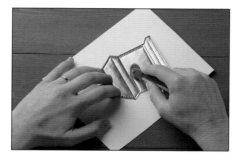

4 Place the decoration face down on a sheet of thin card. Carefully trace over the pen lines with a dressmaker's wheel to emboss a row of raised dots on the front of the decoration. Trace a second line of dots inside the first, in the centre of the decoration.

5 Using the picture as a guide, draw the details of the house on the back of the decoration using a ballpoint pen.

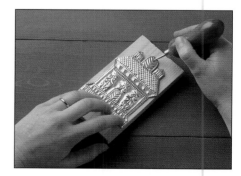

6 Place the decoration face up on a small block of wood. Using a bradawl, carefully make a hole in the top of the decoration. Tie a length of fine wire through the hole to make a hanger.

MATERIALS AND EQUIPMENT YOU WILL NEED

TRACING PAPER • SOFT PENCIL • THIN CARD • SCISSORS • 36 GAUGE (0.005 IN) ALUMINIUM FOIL • SHARP PENCIL •
EMBROIDERY SCISSORS • MARKER PEN • RULER • DRESSMAKER'S WHEEL • BALLPOINT PEN •
WOODEN BLOCK • BRADAWL • FINE WIRE

PAINTED MIRROR

PAINTED TINWARE IS PART OF THE POPULAR ART OF MANY COUNTRIES, PARTICULARLY INDIA AND LATIN AMERICA, WHERE FINE-GAUGE TIN IS STAMPED WITH DECORATIVE PATTERNS AND OFTEN HIGHLIGHTED WITH TRANSLUCENT PAINTS. THIS MIRROR FRAME FOLLOWS THE TRADITION. IT IS PUNCHED FROM BOTH THE BACK AND THE FRONT, WHICH RAISES SOME SECTIONS OF THE METAL TO MAKE A LOW RELIEF SURFACE. THE TRANSLUCENT PAINTS USED TO DECORATE THE FRAME ARE MADE PRIMARILY FOR PAINTING GLASSWARE, BUT ARE SUITABLE FOR USE ON METAL AS WELL. THE PAINT SHOULD BE APPLIED SPARINGLY SO THAT THE SHEEN OF THE TIN IS STILL VISIBLE THROUGH THE COLOURED SURFACE.

1 To make the mirror frame, measure out a 30 cm (12 in) square on a sheet of tin. Draw a 1 cm (½ in) border inside the square. Measure a point 2 cm (¾ in) from each corner of the outer square. Draw diagonal lines from these points to the corners of the smaller square. Wearing a work shirt and protective gloves, cut the square from the sheet of tin with tin shears. Cut along the diagonal lines at the corners.

2 Firmly clamp the 90° block of wood in a bench vice. Place the mirror frame on the wooden block with the ruled edge of the tin resting on the edge of the block. Using a hide hammer, tap along the edge of the tin to turn it over to an angle of 90°.

3 Turn the frame over. Hold the 45° block of wood inside the turned edge and hammer the edge over. Remove the block and hammer the edge completely flat. Finish the remaining three edges of the frame in the same way. Carefully file the corners of the mirror frame to remove any sharp edges.

▶

MATERIALS AND EQUIPMENT YOU WILL NEED

SHEET OF 30 GAUGE (0.01 IN) TIN PLATE • MARKER PEN • RULER • WORK SHIRT AND PROTECTIVE LEATHER GLOVES • TIN SHEARS • 90° AND 45° WOODEN BLOCKS • BENCH VICE • HIDE HAMMER • FILE • GRAPH PAPER • SCISSORS • SAUCER • PENCIL • MASKING TAPE • SHEET OF CHIPBOARD • PANEL PINS • TACK HAMMER • CENTRE PUNCH • BALL HAMMER • CHINAGRAPH PENCIL • SOFT CLOTH • TRANSLUCENT PAINTS • PAINTBRUSH • SQUARE MIRROR TILE • 36 GAUGE (0.005 IN) ALUMINIUM FOIL • EPOXY RESIN GLUE • 40 GAUGE (0.003 IN) COPPER FOIL • D-RING HANGER

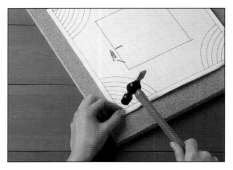

4 Cut a piece of graph paper the same size as the frame. Using a saucer as a template, draw the decorative corner lines on to the paper. Draw in the central square which should be slightly larger than the mirror tile. Tape the pattern to the back of the frame. Lay the frame face down on the chipboard and secure with a panel pins.

5 Place the point of the centre punch on a line of the inside square and tap it with the ball hammer to make an indentation. Move the punch about 3 mm (⅛ in) along the line and tap it to make the next mark. Continue punching along all the lines until the design is completed.

6 Unpin the frame from the board, remove the paper pattern and turn the frame over. Using a chinagraph pencil, draw a square halfway along each edge between the corner decorations. Draw a heart in each square. Pin the frame to the board again and punch an outline around each square and heart. Randomly punch the border between the heart and the square to make a densely pitted surface.

7 Remove the frame from the board. Wipe over the surface of the metal with a soft cloth to remove any grease. Paint the embossed areas of the frame with transluscent paint. Leave the paint to dry thoroughly and apply a second coat if the first is patchy.

8 Lay the mirror tile on aluminium foil and draw around it. Draw a 1.5 cm (⅝ in) border around the outline. Cut out the foil, snipping the corners at right angles.

9 Glue the tile to the centre of the foil. Glue the edges of the foil over the tile. Cut four small squares of copper foil and glue one square in each corner of the tile.

10 Glue the mirror to the centre of the frame. Glue the hanger to the back of the frame. Allow the glue to dry thoroughly before hanging up the mirror.

SPICE RACK

THIS HANDSOME SPICE RACK IS MADE FROM A BISCUIT BOX. UNWANTED FOOD CONTAINERS ARE A GOOD SOURCE OF TIN AND ARE PERFECT FOR THIS SORT OF ITEM, AS THEY ARE ALREADY PARTLY FORMED INTO THE RIGHT SHAPE. SOME TINS ARE BRIGHTLY COLOURED AND, IF YOU DON'T WANT TO INCORPORATE THIS CHARACTERISTIC INTO THE DESIGN OF YOUR FINISHED ITEM, IT IS OFTEN POSSIBLE TO REMOVE THE DECORATION USING PAINT STRIPPER. WEAR PROTECTIVE CLOTHING AND WORK IN A WELL-VENTILATED AREA IF YOU DO THIS.

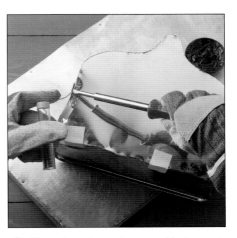

1 Wearing a work shirt and protective gloves, carefully cut the base of the biscuit box in half using tin shears. File all the cut edges smooth.

2 Draw the curved shape of the back panel of the spice rack on to the lid of the box. Cut it out using tin shears. File all the cut edges smooth. Place the back of the spice rack in position against the cut edge of one half of the biscuit box. Hold the two together with strips of masking tape.

3 Place the spice rack on a soldering mat. Wearing a protective mask and goggles, apply flux along the join and solder the two parts together. Carefully turn over the filed edges of the back panel and the base using pliers. Squeeze the turned edges firmly between the pliers to flatten them completely. File any remaining rough edges smooth.

▶

MATERIALS AND EQUIPMENT YOU WILL NEED

WORK SHIRT AND PROTECTIVE LEATHER GLOVES • BISCUIT BOX • TIN SHEARS • FILE • MARKER PEN • MASKING TAPE • SCISSORS • SOLDERING MAT • FLUX • PROTECTIVE MASK AND GOGGLES • SOLDERING IRON AND SOLDER • PLIERS • RULER OR TAPE MEASURE • FINE WIRE • WIRE CUTTERS • WOODEN BLOCK • BRADAWL • SCRAP OF BRASS SHIM • SUPER GLUE

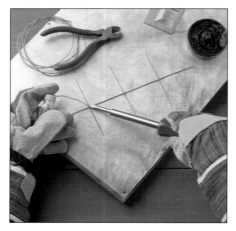

4 Measure the dimensions of the inside of the spice rack. Cut lengths of fine wire and solder them together to make a grid to form compartments for the spice bottles.

5 Place the grid inside the spice rack and carefully solder it in place.

6 Place the top edge of the rack on a block of wood and pierce a hole in it using a bradawl. Open the hole slightly using a pair of pliers. File away the rough edges around the inside of the hole. Turn over the edges around the hole and squeeze them flat using the pliers.

7 Cut a long length of fine wire and curve it into a spiral shape using pliers. Cut six lengths of wire and form two large and two small curves and two small circles. Solder the spiral to the back of the rack and the curves to the front. Shape a piece of wire to fit around the edges of the back of the tin and solder it in place.

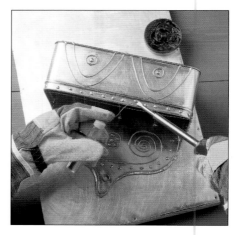

8 Cut a small circle of shim and glue it to the centre back of the rack. Apply decorative blobs of solder to the shim circle, along the edges of the rack and around the wire spiral and curves.

NUMBER PLAQUE

THE RISING SUN, A VERY POPULAR DOMESTIC ART DECO MOTIF IN THE 1930s, HAS BEEN INCORPORATED INTO THE DESIGN OF THIS DOOR NUMBER PLAQUE. INDENTATIONS ARE PUNCHED INTO THE FRONT OF THE PLAQUE TO CREATE A DENSELY PITTED, DEPRESSED SURFACE IN THE TIN AND TO RAISE THE UNPUNCHED AREAS SLIGHTLY. THIS IS A SIMPLE FORM OF CHASING, AN ANCIENT METALWORKING TECHNIQUE WHERE DEFINITION IS GIVEN TO A DECORATIVE DESIGN BY RAISING AND INDENTING AREAS OF THE METAL SO THAT THE DESIGN STANDS OUT IN RELIEF. AFTER THE DESIGN HAS BEEN PUNCHED INTO THE PLAQUE, THE SURFACE OF THE TIN IS SCOURED WITH WIRE WOOL TO GIVE A MORE MATT FINISH.

1 Draw a rectangle on a sheet of tin. Draw a 1 cm (½ in) border around the inside of the rectangle. Measure a point 2.5 cm (1 in) from each corner of the outer rectangle. Draw diagonal lines across the corners. Wearing protective clothing, cut out the plaque.

3 Turn the plaque over and position the 45° wooden block inside the turned edge. Hammer the edge over it, remove the block and then hammer the edge completely flat. Finish the remaining three sides of the plaque in the same way. Carefully file the corners to make them smooth.

5 Place the centre punch on a line and tap it with a ball hammer to make an indentation. Move the punch about 3 mm (⅛ in) along the line and tap it again to make the next mark. Continue to punch along the lines until the design is completed.

2 Firmly clamp the 90° block of wood in a bench vice. Place the plaque on the wooden block with the ruled edge of the tin resting on the edge of the block. Using a hide hammer, tap along the edge of the plaque to turn it over to an angle of 90°.

4 Cut a piece of graph paper the same size as the plaque. Draw in your pattern and desired numbers. Tape the pattern to the front of the plaque. Secure it to the chipboard with a panel pin in each corner.

6 Remove the paper pattern, then randomly punch the surface around the sunburst and inside the numbers. Scour the surface of the panel with wire wool before sealing the plaque with varnish.

MATERIALS AND EQUIPMENT YOU WILL NEED

SHEET OF 30 GAUGE (0.01 IN) TIN PLATE • MARKER PEN • RULER • WORK SHIRT AND PROTECTIVE LEATHER GLOVES • TIN SHEARS •
90° AND 45° WOODEN BLOCKS • BENCH VICE • HIDE HAMMER • FILE • GRAPH PAPER • PENCIL • MASKING TAPE • SHEET OF CHIPBOARD •
PANEL PINS • TACK HAMMER • CENTRE PUNCH • BALL HAMMER • WIRE WOOL • CLEAR POLYURETHANE VARNISH • PAINTBRUSH

REINDEER

THIS CHARMING REINDEER IS MADE FROM ZINC PLATE THAT IS THIN ENOUGH TO CURVE AND MANIPULATE EASILY. ZINC PLATE IS STEEL THAT HAS BEEN COATED WITH A THIN LAYER OF ZINC TO PROTECT IT FROM CORROSION. THIS GIVES THE METAL AN ATTRACTIVE MATT APPEARANCE. ZINC PLATE IS AVAILABLE FROM HARDWARE STORES, METAL MERCHANTS AND BUILDING SUPPLIERS IN VARIOUS WEIGHTS. CHOOSE A THIN GAUGE AS YOU WILL NEED TO BEND THE METAL. TAKE EXTRA CARE WHEN SOLDERING THE REINDEER, AS ZINC CAN GIVE OFF NOXIOUS FUMES WHEN IT IS HEATED. WEAR A FACE MASK AND GOGGLES AS USUAL AND WORK IN A VERY WELL-VENTILATED AREA, TAKING FREQUENT BREAKS.

1 Trace the head and body templates from page 92, enlarge them if necessary, and transfer them to thin card. Cut out the shapes to make templates. Draw around each template on to a sheet of thin zinc plate using a marker pen. Wearing a work shirt and protective gloves, cut out the head and body using tin snips. Carefully file all the edges and the corners to make them completely smooth. Draw and cut out two ears.

2 Place a paintbrush in the middle of each leg and the tail and gently tap it with a small hammer to curve the metal and make a cylinder. Curve the reindeer's body. The reindeer will now stand upright. Lay the reindeer on a soldering mat and apply flux to the joins. Wearing a protective mask and goggles, spot solder along the inside of each leg and the body.

3 Take the head piece and gently curve the reindeer's neck to make a cylinder. Hold the edges together with masking tape while you spot solder along the join. Gently bend the head downwards and curve the sides to make it cylindrical.

►

MATERIALS AND EQUIPMENT YOU WILL NEED

TRACING PAPER • SOFT PENCIL • THIN CARD • SCISSORS • THIN ZINC PLATE • MARKER PEN •
WORK SHIRT AND PROTECTIVE LEATHER GLOVES • TIN SNIPS • FILE • PAINTBRUSHES • SMALL HAMMER • SOLDERING MAT • FLUX •
PROTECTIVE MASK AND GOGGLES • SOLDERING IRON AND SOLDER • MASKING TAPE • FINE WIRE • WIRE CUTTERS •
PLIERS • ENAMEL PAINTS

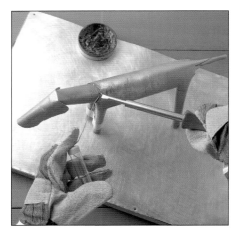

4 Place the head section inside the body. Wrap a strip of masking tape around the two front legs to pull them tightly together so that the head fits snugly inside the body. Solder along the join where the neck meets the body.

5 To make the reindeer's antlers, cut two long pieces of fine wire and 14 shorter pieces. Bend the shorter pieces into diamond shapes. Solder the wire diamonds to the two long pieces of wire. Using masking tape to keep them in place, solder the antlers to the sides of the reindeer's head. Reshape them after soldering to make them slightly irregular.

6 Gently curve the reindeer's ears and solder them to its head next to the antlers. Hold them in position with small pieces of masking tape while you work.

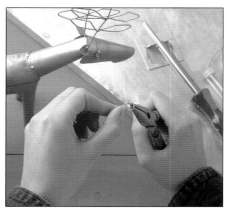

7 To make the reindeer's eyes, cut two short pieces of wire and twist them around the end of a pair of pliers to make spirals. Solder the reindeer's eyes to the sides of the head.

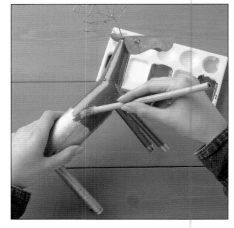

8 Paint the reindeer, except for its antlers, with two coats of red enamel paint, allowing the first coat to dry before adding the second.

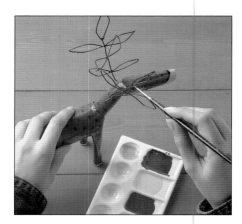

9 When the red paint is dry, paint blue spots on the reindeer's body. Paint its ears, hooves, nose and tail yellow. Paint a black line around the nose and the hooves and paint the reindeer's antlers blue.

BATHROOM SHELF

THIS CLASSIC BATHROOM SHELF IS CONSTRUCTED VERY SIMPLY FROM MDF, WHICH CAN BE PRIMED AND PAINTED IN THE SAME WAY AS WOOD. IT IS ADORNED WITH TIN FISH AND SHELL CUT-OUTS THAT HAVE BEEN PUNCHED FROM THE BACK TO GIVE A LOW-RELIEF DECORATIVE SURFACE. TIN PLATE IS SUITABLE FOR AREAS WHERE WATER IS PRESENT, AS THE TIN COATING PREVENTS THE METAL FROM TARNISHING IN DAMP, STEAMY CONDITIONS. A MIRROR IS STUCK TO THE SHELF TO ADD TO THE DECORATION. THIS SHELF IS ATTACHED TO THE BATHROOM WALL USING MIRROR PLATES AND SO SHOULD ONLY BE USED TO SUPPORT LIGHTWEIGHT OBJECTS SUCH AS TOOTHBRUSH MUGS AND SHAVING EQUIPMENT.

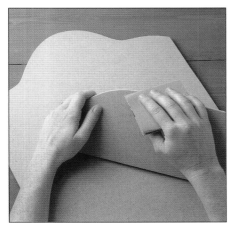

1 Draw out the templates for the back and ledge of the bathroom shelf on to squared graph paper to make a pattern for each. The back is 40 cm (16 in) high at the sides and 30 cm (12 in) wide. The ledge is the same width as the back and 15 cm (6 in) deep at its widest point. Cut out the patterns and draw around them on to the sheet of MDF. Saw out the shapes and smooth the edges using fine sandpaper.

2 Measure the outside dimensions of the mirror tile. Cut four lengths of battening strip to make a recess for the tile. Using strong wood glue, attach the battening strips to the panel. Pin the corners with small panel pins for extra strength. Glue and pin the ledge to the bottom edge of the back panel.

3 Seal the surface of the bathroom shelf with one coat of wood primer. Lightly sand the surface of the shelf and paint it with satin-finish wood paint.

▶

MATERIALS AND EQUIPMENT YOU WILL NEED

PENCIL • GRAPH PAPER • SCISSORS • SHEET OF 10 MM (½ IN) MDF (MEDIUM-DENSITY FIBREBOARD) • HANDSAW •
FINE SANDPAPER • MIRROR TILE • RULER • 25 x 5 MM (1 x ³⁄₁₆ IN) BATTENING STRIPS • WOOD GLUE • PANEL PINS •
TACK HAMMER • WOOD PRIMER • PAINTBRUSH • SATIN-FINISH WOOD PAINT • TRACING PAPER • THIN CARD •
WORK SHIRT AND PROTECTIVE LEATHER GLOVES • 30 GAUGE (0.01 IN) TIN PLATE • FINE MARKER PEN • TIN SNIPS •
BENCH VICE • SMALL FILE • WET AND DRY PAPER • WOODEN BLOCK • CHINAGRAPH PENCIL •
SHEET OF CHIPBOARD • MASKING TAPE • CENTRE PUNCH • BALL HAMMER • EPOXY RESIN GLUE • 2 MIRROR PLATES

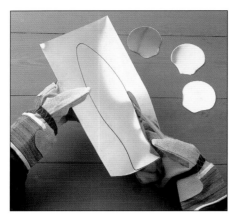

4 Trace the fish and shell templates from page 92, enlarging them if necessary. Transfer them to thin card and cut them out. Wearing a work shirt and protective leather gloves, cut pieces of tin plate approximately the same size as the templates. Draw around the templates on to the tin using a fine marker pen. Draw one fish and five shells. Carefully cut out the fish and shell shapes using tin snips.

5 Clamp each shape firmly in a bench vice. Using a small file, work around each shape removing any metal burrs and rough edges. Finish off the edges with a damp piece of wet and dry paper, wrapped around a wooden block. They should be perfectly smooth with no sharp edges.

6 Draw in the decorative designs on the back of each shell and the fish with a chinagraph pencil.

7 Tape the fish and shells face down on to a sheet of chipboard. Place the centre punch on a line and tap it with the ball hammer to make an indentation. Continue punching along the lines, leaving about 3 mm (⅛ in) between each indentation. Punch designs into the shells in the same way.

8 Lay the fish and shell shapes in position around the bathroom shelf. Attach them to the shelf using panel pins and a tack hammer.

9 Using epoxy resin glue, stick the mirror tile into the recess in the shelf back. Press the tile firmly into place. Let the glue dry thoroughly, then screw a mirror plate to either side of the shelf.

EMBOSSED BOOK JACKET

THE APPEARANCE OF A PLAIN NOTEBOOK OR PHOTOGRAPH ALBUM CAN BE DRAMATICALLY ENHANCED WITH AN EMBOSSED METAL PANEL. THE PANEL COVERING THIS BOOK IMITATES THE ORNATE LEATHER AND METAL BINDINGS ADORNING EARLY BIBLES AND PRAYER BOOKS. THESE WERE OFTEN STUDDED WITH SEMI-PRECIOUS STONES, A LOOK THAT CAN BE ACHIEVED BY USING COLOURED GLASS CABOCHONS, AVAILABLE FROM JEWELLER'S SUPPLIERS. GOLD LACQUER PAINT HAS BEEN USED TO HIGHLIGHT SMALL AREAS OF THE EMBOSSED PATTERN TO GIVE IT A RICH, BYZANTINE FEEL. SIMPLE TEMPLATES ARE USED TO EMBOSS THE BASIC PATTERN INTO THE PANEL, THEN MORE DETAIL IS ADDED FREEHAND.

1 Cut a piece of aluminium foil the same size as the front of the book. Using a soft marker pen and a ruler, draw a 5 mm (³⁄₁₆ in) border all the way around the edge of the foil. Divide the rectangle into squares. Using a ruler and ballpoint pen, redraw over the lines to emboss the foil. This is now the back of the jacket.

2 Draw a circle and a rectangle on to card. They should be small enough to fit into the grid squares. Then draw another slightly smaller circle and square. Cut out the shapes.

3 Place the larger round template in the centre of the first square. Carefully draw around it using a ballpoint pen. Repeat with the larger rectangle in the next square. Alternate the shapes to cover the whole jacket.

4 Lay the smaller round template inside the embossed circles and draw around it. Place the smaller rectangle template inside the larger rectangles and emboss all the shapes in the same way.

5 Draw a small double circle and double semi-circles inside each circle. Draw a double oval and radiating lines inside each rectangle. Emboss a dotted line around each rectangle and around the edge of the jacket.

6 Turn the jacket over so that it is face up. Using a fine brush, highlight small areas of the design with gold lacquer paint. When the paint is thoroughly dry, glue the jacket to the front of the book.

MATERIALS AND EQUIPMENT YOU WILL NEED

SHEET OF 36 GAUGE (0.005 IN) ALUMINIUM FOIL • SCISSORS • SOFT MARKER PEN • RULER • BALLPOINT PEN •
PENCIL • THIN CARD • FINE PAINTBRUSH • GOLD LACQUER PAINT • EPOXY RESIN GLUE

HERB CONTAINER

THIS BRIGHTLY PAINTED HERB CONTAINER IS MADE FROM RECYCLED TIN CANS THAT ARE HAMMERED FLAT AND SOLDERED TOGETHER TO MAKE A BOX. THE TOP EDGES ARE BOUND WITH FINE WIRE AND WIRE IS ALSO USED TO MAKE SEEDS AND PETALS FOR THE FLOWERS. THE CONTAINER HAS AN APPEALING FOLK ART BRIGHTNESS AND CHARM THAT WOULD SIT WELL IN ANY KITCHEN. PUNCHED HOLES IN THE BOTTOM ALLOW FOR WATER DRAINAGE AND THE BOX WILL HOLD THREE SMALL POTS OF HERBS QUITE COMFORTABLY. THE CONTAINER IS FOR INSIDE USE ONLY. IT IS SOMETHING THAT WOULD LOOK GOOD STANDING ON A SUNNY WINDOW SILL FOR A READY SUPPLY OF FRESH HERBS.

1 Using a tin opener, remove the tops and bottoms from four tin cans. Wearing a work shirt and protective gloves, cut the tins open down one side using tin shears. Place the tin panels on a sheet of chipboard and flatten them using a hide hammer. File all the edges of the tins to make them completely smooth.

2 Use one flattened piece of tin to make the base. Bend the other three tins around the base to make a box shape. Hold all the sections of the box together with strips of masking tape. Place the box on a soldering mat, apply flux to the join and, wearing a protective mask and goggles, solder the sections together.

3 Cut four strips of thin tin plate the same length as the sides of the box base and file the edges smooth. Lay each strip along the edge of a long block of wood and hammer it over to make a right angle along its length.

MATERIALS AND EQUIPMENT YOU WILL NEED

TIN OPENER • 4 TIN CANS • WORK SHIRT AND PROTECTIVE LEATHER GLOVES • TIN SHEARS • SHEET OF CHIPBOARD • HIDE HAMMER • FILE • MASKING TAPE • PROTECTIVE MASK AND GOGGLES • SOLDERING MAT • FLUX • SOLDERING IRON AND SOLDER • THIN TIN PLATE • BLOCK OF WOOD • SMALL HAMMER • BRADAWL • FINE WIRE • WIRE CUTTERS • PLIERS • CLOTHES PEGS • ENAMEL PAINTS • PAINTBRUSH

4 Solder the strips of tin around the base of the box and then carefully file all the corners to remove any sharp edges. Using a bradawl, punch two holes in the bottom of the box for drainage and file around the holes to remove the rough edges.

5 Cut three lengths of fine wire long enough to fit around the sides and front of the top of the box. Bend the pieces of wire to the same shape as the box and solder them together.

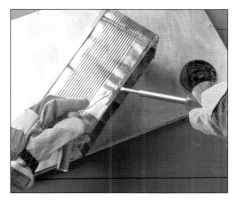

6 Solder the wires around the side and front edges of the top of the box.

7 To make the flower heads, cut three circles of thin tin about the same size as the tops of the cans. File all the edges smooth. Cut short lengths of wire and twist them around the end of a pair of pliers to make seed shapes.

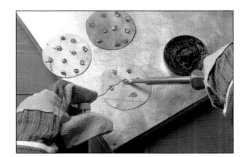

8 Place the seeds on the flower heads. Drop a dot of solder in the centre of each seed to join it to the head.

9 Solder the flower heads to the back of the box. Hold them in position using clothes pegs as you work.

10 Cut three lengths of wire long enough to fit around the flower heads. Using your fingers, make long loops of wire for petals. Solder the petals at equal distances along each length of wire.

▶

11 Bend the wire petals around the flower heads and solder them to the back of the box. Use pegs to keep the petals in position while you work.

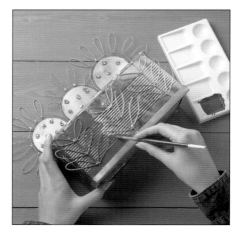

13 Solder the stems to the front and sides of the box. Paint the box using blue enamel paint.

12 To make the flower stems, cut five lengths of wire the same height as the front and sides of the container. Use your fingers to make six wire leaf shapes for each stem. Solder the leaves to the stems.

14 When the blue paint has dried, paint the stems white and the petals red. Paint the flower heads yellow and paint the seeds black. Paint the strip around the base of the box red.

WALL SCONCE

THIS SIMPLE, ELEGANT SCONCE IS MADE FROM SMALL FLUTED PUDDING MOULDS. THE SHINY RIPPLED SURFACES REFLECT AND INTENSIFY THE CANDLELIGHT BEAUTIFULLY. CATERING SUPPLIERS STOCK ALL SORTS OF MOULDS FOR CONFECTIONERY, BISCUITS AND CAKES, AND LOTS OF INTERESTING SHAPES ARE AVAILABLE. THE MOULDS ARE VERY SIMPLY JOINED USING FINE WIRE AND POP RIVETS AND A WIRE LOOP IS ADDED TO SUSPEND THE SCONCE FROM THE WALL. NIGHT LIGHTS AND CANDLES CAN BE A FIRE HAZARD AND SHOULD NEVER BE LEFT TO BURN UNATTENDED.

1 Wearing a work shirt and protective gloves, cut a 20 cm (8 in) strip of thin tin about 7 mm (¼ in) wider than the base of the scallop mould. Carefully turn over and flatten the long sides of the strip using pliers. File the corners smooth.

2 Place the tin strip on a block of wood. Hold the edge with pliers and drill two holes in one end of the strip. File the holes smooth. Bend forward the lip of the scallop mould using pliers. Place the tin strip on the lip and mark where the holes are. Drill holes in the mould and file them smooth.

3 Line up the holes in the mould and the tin strip and pop rivet the two together.

4 Using pliers, bend the tin strip down, then outwards to make a shelf. Hold the oval mould on the block of wood with pliers and drill two holes in the bottom. File the holes smooth.

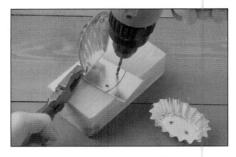

5 Place the mould on the shelf and mark where the edge of the mould comes to and the position of the holes. Drill two holes in the shelf and file the edges smooth. Cut off the excess tin strip and file the edge smooth. Pop rivet the mould to the shelf.

6 Pierce two holes in the back of the sconce. File the holes smooth. To make a hanger, cut a length of fine wire. Make a coil in one end, then pass the uncoiled end through the sconce. Make a loop, then pass the wire back through. Make a second coil and cut off the wire.

MATERIALS AND EQUIPMENT YOU WILL NEED

WORK SHIRT AND PROTECTIVE LEATHER GLOVES • PIECE OF 30 GAUGE (0.01 IN) TIN PLATE • SCALLOP MOULD AND OVAL MOULD • TIN SHEARS • PLIERS • FILE • WOODEN BLOCK • DRILL • POP RIVETER AND RIVETS • MARKER PEN • BRADAWL • FINE WIRE • WIRE CUTTERS • ROUND-NOSED PLIERS

REGAL COAT RACK

A COAT RACK WILL KEEP COATS, UMBRELLAS AND HATS TIDY, AVOIDING CLUTTER IN HALLS AND DOORWAYS. THE RICH PURPLE BACKGROUND AND THE SLIGHTLY MATT TONES OF THE METAL FOILS GIVE THIS RACK A TOUCH OF MEDIEVAL SPLENDOUR WITH GOTHIC OVERTONES THAT WOULD SIT WELL WITH PARQUET OR TILED FLOORING AND CAST-IRON LIGHT FITTINGS. THE BASIC SHAPE CAN EASILY BE ADAPTED TO MAKE A UTENSIL RACK FOR THE KITCHEN OR A TOWEL RAIL FOR THE BATHROOM. A KITCHEN RACK SHOULD IDEALLY HAVE LOTS OF EVENLY SPACED HOOKS TO HANG LADLES, WHISKS, SIEVES AND SO ON, WHILE A BATHROOM RACK COULD HAVE WOODEN PEGS RATHER THAN METAL HOOKS.

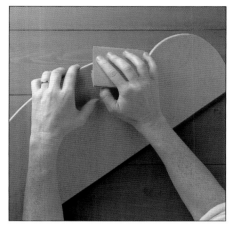

1 Draw the basic shape for the coat rack on to squared graph paper to make a pattern. This rack is 60 cm (23½ in) wide and 20 cm (8 in) high at its highest point. Cut out the pattern and draw around it on to the sheet of MDF. Saw out the shape and then smooth the edges using fine sandpaper.

2 Seal the surface of the coat rack with one coat of wood primer. Lightly sand the surface of the coat rack and paint it with satin-finish wood paint.

3 Trace the crown, fleur-de-lys and star templates from page 93, enlarge them if necessary, then transfer them on to a sheet of thin card. Cut the shapes out to make templates. ▶

MATERIALS AND EQUIPMENT YOU WILL NEED

PENCIL • GRAPH PAPER • SCISSORS • SHEET OF 6 MM (¼ IN) MDF (MEDIUM-DENSITY FIBREBOARD) • HANDSAW • FINE SANDPAPER • WOOD PRIMER • PAINTBRUSH • SATIN-FINISH WOOD PAINT • TRACING PAPER • SOFT PENCIL • THIN CARD • 40 GAUGE (0.003 IN) COPPER FOIL • BALLPOINT PEN • 36 GAUGE (0.005 IN) ALUMINIUM FOIL • CENTRE PUNCH • EPOXY RESIN GLUE • DRILL • 3 BALL END HOOKS • 2 MIRROR PLATES

4 Lay the crown template on a piece of copper foil. Draw around the template on to the foil using a ballpoint pen. Repeat to make a second crown. Draw around the fleur-de-lys and stars on to a sheet of aluminium foil. Draw two stars. Cut out all the shapes using scissors.

5 Rest each foil shape on a piece of thin card. Make a line of dots around the edge of each shape by pressing into the foil using a centre punch.

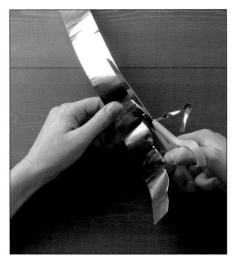

6 Cut a 5 cm (2 in) wide strip of aluminium foil the same length as the bottom edge of the coat rack. Cut a wavy line along the top edge of the strip and then mark a row of dots along it with the punch.

7 Place the wavy edging and the stars, crowns and fleur-de-lys on the front of the coat rack with the raised side of the dots facing upwards. Use epoxy resin glue to stick all the pieces in position.

8 When the glue has dried thoroughly, drill three holes at equal distances 2.5 cm (1 in) from the bottom edge of the coat rack. Screw a hook into each hole. Attach a mirror plate to either side of the coat rack for hanging.

TIN CAN CHANDELIER

THIS CHANDELIER IS MADE FROM EIGHT SMALL TIN CANS AND A TIN FLAN RING. IT IS VERY SIMPLE IN CONSTRUCTION, BUT LOOKS VERY EFFECTIVE WHEN FILLED WITH FLICKERING NIGHT LIGHTS. THE TIN CANS ARE COLOURED GOLD ON THE INSIDE WHICH INTENSIFIES THE LIGHT. THE CHANDELIER IS SUSPENDED FROM STRONG BEADED CHAIN. MAKE SURE YOU BUY THE KIND WITH FORGED LINKS THAT CAN WITHSTAND THE WEIGHT OF THE CHANDELIER. GLASS NUGGETS ARE USED TO DECORATE THE OUTSIDE OF THE CHANDELIER, GIVING IT AN ECCLESIASTICAL AIR REMINISCENT OF A CORONA, A LARGE CHANDELIER THAT IS SUSPENDED FROM CHURCH CEILINGS. THE CHANDELIER IS DESIGNED TO HOLD NIGHT LIGHTS AND SHOULD NOT BE USED WITH CANDLES. NIGHT LIGHTS CAN BE A FIRE HAZARD AND SHOULD NEVER BE LEFT TO BURN UNATTENDED.

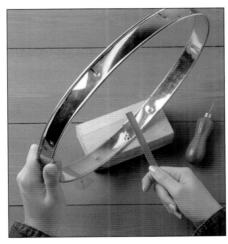

1 Measure and mark eight evenly spaced points around the flan ring. Rest the ring on a block of wood and pierce a hole at each point using a bradawl. File away the rough edges at the back of the holes.

2 Mark three equally spaced points around the top of the ring. Pierce them with a bradawl as before and file away the rough edges.

3 Using a tin opener, remove the top from each tin and file the edges smooth. Measure and mark a point halfway down each tin can (avoiding the seam in the can). Clamp a length of wooden pole in a bench vice. Support each can on the pole and pierce a hole in the side at the marked point using a bradawl. File away the rough edges around the holes.

▶

MATERIALS AND EQUIPMENT YOU WILL NEED

TAPE MEASURE • MARKER PEN • TIN FLAN RING, 30 CM (12 IN) IN DIAMETER • WOODEN BLOCK • BRADAWL • FILE • TIN OPENER • 8 SMALL TINS • LENGTH OF WOODEN POLE • BENCH VICE • 8 NUTS AND SHORT BOLTS • SCREWDRIVER • 4 S-JOINERS • PLIERS • STRONG BEADED CHAIN • WIRE CUTTERS • 4 JUMP RINGS • KEY RING • EPOXY RESIN GLUE • COLOURED GLASS NUGGETS

4 Place each can against a hole in the flan ring. Join the cans to the ring using short bolts. Screw the nuts on to the bolts as tightly as they will go to keep the tins firmly in position.

6 Cut three 30 cm (12 in) lengths of beaded chain. Attach a jump ring to the end of each chain length, then attach a length to each S-joiner. Close the jump rings very tightly using pliers.

8 Glue green glass nuggets around the outside of the chandelier. Glue a red glass nugget to the outside of each tin.

5 Attach an S-joiner through each of the three holes in the top of the flan ring. Using pliers, close the joiners as tightly as they will go.

7 Hold the free ends of the chains together and join them using a jump ring. Join the jump ring to an S-joiner and close the ring very tightly. Attach a key ring to the top of the S-joiner to make a hanger.

JEWELLERY BOX

THIN ZINC SHEET IS QUITE MALLEABLE AND CAN BE USED AS A DECORATIVE CLADDING FOR ALL SORTS OF ITEMS. IT HAS A SUBTLE SHEEN RATHER LIKE PEWTER. BRASS SHIM IS A FAIRLY SOFT METAL USED MOSTLY BY SCULPTORS. IT CAN BE CUT WITH TIN SHEARS OR SNIPS. THE TWO METALS GO WELL TOGETHER AND THIS JEWELLERY BOX HAS A SUBTLE HERALDIC SPLENDOUR THAT IS UNDERLINED BY THE DECORATIVE BLOBS OF SOLDER RESEMBLING METAL STUDS. LOOK OUT FOR OLD CIGAR BOXES, AS THEY HAVE PLEASING PROPORTIONS AND ARE EASILY OBTAINABLE.

1 Wearing protective clothing, cut a piece of zinc slightly larger than the lid of the cigar box using tin shears. Carefully file any rough edges or burrs of metal.

2 Draw a diamond and two different-sized hearts on a sheet of thin card and cut them out. Lay the templates on a piece of shim and draw around them – six small hearts, one large heart and two diamonds. Draw some small circles freehand. Draw one small heart on a scrap of zinc. Cut out all the shapes and file the edges smooth. Place them on a sheet of chipboard and stamp a line of dots around each using a hammer and nail. Do not stamp the circles and zinc heart.

3 Cut four thin strips of shim to make a border around the zinc panel. Place all the pieces on a soldering mat and, wearing a protective mask and goggles, drop a blob of liquid solder in the centre of the circles, small hearts and diamonds. Cover the zinc heart with solder blobs. Add a line of blobs to each piece of the shim border.

4 Stick all the shapes and the borders on the zinc panel, leaving a small rim around the outside of the borders to turn down over the sides of the box. Turn the rim down.

5 Cut a strip of zinc as wide as the side of the box and long enough to fit all the way around. File the edges smooth. Cut circles of shim, decorate each with a blob of solder and glue them to the strip.

6 Glue the zinc strip around the sides of the box. Glue the zinc panel to the top of the lid. Gently tap along the edges of the panel to turn them over the side of the lid.

MATERIALS AND EQUIPMENT YOU WILL NEED
WORK SHIRT AND PROTECTIVE LEATHER GLOVES • THIN ZINC PLATE • TIN SHEARS • OLD CIGAR BOX • FILE • PENCIL • THIN CARD •
SCISSORS • BRASS SHIM • SHEET OF CHIPBOARD • HAMMER AND NAIL • SOLDERING MAT • PROTECTIVE MASK AND GOGGLES •
SOLDERING IRON AND SOLDER • SUPER GLUE

LUNCH BOX

WITH ITS DISTINCTIVE CURVED LID, THIS LUNCH BOX IS BASED ON TRADITIONAL AMERICAN DESIGNS. THE EXTRA SPACE UNDER THE LID MAKES A HANDY COMPARTMENT FOR STORING DRINKS FLASKS, WHICH LIE ON TOP OF THE FOOD. THE USE OF RECYCLED TIN CANS FOR HOUSEHOLD OBJECTS AND TOYS IS PREVALENT IN PARTS OF AFRICA AND INDIA, WHERE SCRAP METAL IS CAREFULLY COLLECTED AND RECYCLED.

ITEMS OF IMMENSE INGENUITY AND ELEGANCE ARE MADE BY ALL AGE GROUPS, INCLUDING CHILDREN. LOOK OUTSIDE RESTAURANTS AND CAFÉS TO FIND DISCARDED OIL DRUMS AND TINS. CIRCULAR DRUMS ARE THE MOST USEFUL, AS THEY PROVIDE LARGE AREAS OF SMOOTH METAL. TRY TO FIND CONTAINERS PRINTED WITH INTERESTING TEXT OR PICTURES AS SOME ARE VERY ATTRACTIVE AND WILL ENHANCE YOUR FINISHED OBJECT.

1 Wearing a work shirt and protective gloves, cut one end from an oil drum using a hacksaw (see Basic Techniques). Using tin shears, cut open the drum and remove the other end to leave a metal panel. Wipe any excess oil from the panel.

2 Mark out the dimensions of the box cover following the diagram on page 93. Using tin shears, cut out the cover. Carefully cut along the centre of the cover to separate the two sections then snip up the short lines along each side to make the hinges. File away all the rough edges to make the cover safe. Make two small "V"-shaped cuts along each side as shown in the diagram.

3 Firmly clamp the 90° block of wood in the bench vice. Place the cover on the wooden block and carefully turn over one edge using a hide hammer. Turn the cover over. Position the 45° wooden block inside the turned edge and hammer the edge over it. Remove the block and hammer the edge completely flat. Repeat to turn over the other two edges. File all corners of the cover smooth. Repeat this process with the second cover section.

4 Using pliers, turn alternate tabs of the hinges over. Turn the tabs on each of the two covers so that each folded tab is opposite an unfolded tab. Flatten the tabs using a hammer.

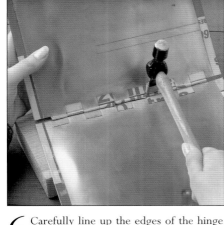

6 Carefully line up the edges of the hinge and link the remaining tabs around the wire to join the two sides. Hammer the tabs under the wire as before, to finish off the hinge.

8 Cut two end blocks using the template as a guide. Place the blocks in position, mark where the top of the sides of the lunch box comes to then saw along this line. Stain the wood red. Fit the case locks.

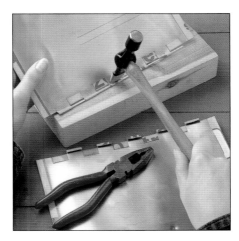

5 Bend half of each unflattened tab back using pliers. Cut a piece of fine wire the same length as the hinge and insert it through the tabs of one of the covers. Hammer the edges of the tabs on this cover firmly under the wire to secure them.

7 Place the cover on a wooden block. Hold the edge of the cover with pliers and drill a small hole 2.5 cm (1 in) in from the edge and each fold line. File the holes smooth. Place the 90° wooden block inside the cover along a fold line and clamp the two together. Gently bend the cover over the block to crease it. Repeat to make a crease along the other fold lines.

9 Separate the blocks and semi-circles and place the blocks inside the cover. Using a bradawl, mark the nail positions on the blocks through the holes. Nail the cover to the blocks.

▶

10 Place the semi-circles of MDF on top of the blocks and close the catches to hold them together. Press the lid around the semi-circles and nail the top and sides of the cover to the semi-circles.

12 Place the handle on top of the lunch box. Using a marker pen, transfer the position of the holes in the handle to the top of the lunch box and drill through. File the holes smooth, then bolt the handle in place, holding the nut firmly from the inside of the box with pliers.

11 Remove the handle from the oil drum. Place it on a wooden block and drill a hole in either end of the handle. File the holes smooth.

ROCKET CANDLESTICK

THIS ALUMINIUM CANDLESTICK HAS A CARTOON-LIKE APPEARANCE THAT IS VERY APPEALING. THE SMALL SECTIONS ARE CONSTRUCTED FIRST AND THEN JOINED TOGETHER. EACH SECTION IS ATTACHED TO THE NEXT USING POP RIVETS. THESE MAKE A STRONG JOINT AS WELL AS BEING DECORATIVE. BECAUSE THE ALUMINIUM IS SOFT, IT IS EASY TO SHAPE USING YOUR HANDS. THE FEET OF THE CANDLESTICK ARE MADE OF OVEN-HARDENING CLAY, WHICH CAN BE PURCHASED FROM CRAFT SHOPS. CANDLES CAN BE A FIRE HAZARD AND SHOULD NEVER BE LEFT TO BURN UNATTENDED.

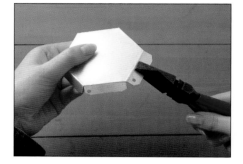

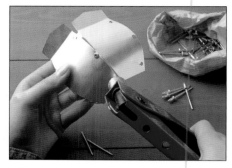

1 Trace and transfer the rocket section templates on page 91 to thin card, enlarging if necessary. Cut out the templates and draw around them on to the aluminium. Draw six side sections, three fins and one top shelf. Wearing a work shirt and protective gloves, cut out all the pieces using tin snips and file the edges smooth. Mark the drilling points on each piece and drill the holes. Hold the metal with a pair of pliers to stop it spinning around while you drill.

2 Using a pair of pliers, carefully fold down all the sides of the top shelf to make an angle of 90°.

4 Hold two side sections together with the tabs to the inside. Join the sections with pop rivets at the middle and bottom holes. Join another two sections in the same way.

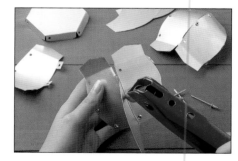

3 Place the side sections on the edge of the wooden block and hammer over the edges. Hold each section in your hands and gently curve it outwards.

5 Place a fin section between two side sections and pop rivet all three together at the middle and bottom holes. Pop rivet the other fins and side sections together.

MATERIALS AND EQUIPMENT YOU WILL NEED
TRACING PAPER • SOFT PENCIL • THIN CARD • SCISSORS • THIN ALUMINIUM SHEET • WORK SHIRT AND PROTECTIVE LEATHER GLOVES •
TIN SNIPS • FILE • DRILL • PLIERS • 90° WOODEN BLOCK • HAMMER • POP RIVETER AND RIVETS • BLACK OVEN-HARDENING CLAY •
EPOXY RESIN GLUE

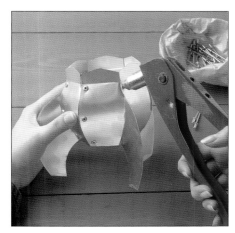

6 Position the shelf at the top of the candlestick with the sides pointing downwards. Join the shelf to the base with pop rivets through the top holes.

7 To make the candlestick feet, roll three balls of black oven-hardening clay. Flatten the base of each one and make an indentation in the top. Bake the clay according to the manufacturer's instructions. When the clay is cool, glue a foot to the end of each fin.

PLANT MARKERS

THESE SIMPLE PLANT MARKERS WILL LEND AN AIR OF ELEGANT ORDER TO ANY SEED BED OR CONTAINER, AND MAKE A NICE CHANGE FROM PLASTIC MARKERS. THEY ARE VERY SIMPLE IN CONSTRUCTION AND WILL HOLD TOGETHER WITHOUT ANY GLUE. THEY ARE MADE FROM COPPER FOIL WHICH, IF THE MARKERS ARE USED OUTDOORS, WILL CHANGE COLOUR TO A DELICATE VERDIGRIS AS IT REACTS TO THE ELEMENTS. LATIN PLANT NAMES ARE PUNCHED INTO EACH MARKER BUT YOU CAN USE THE COMMON NAME FOR EACH PLANT IF YOU PREFER.

1 Trace the template on page 94 and transfer it to thin card enlarging as necessary. Cut out the template and draw around it on to a sheet of copper foil.

2 Cut the marker from the sheet of foil using a pair of scissors.

3 Place the copper marker on a sheet of thin card on top of a sheet of chipboard. Carefully punch the design and plant name into the front of the marker using a bradawl.

4 Cut all the way up the stem along the line directly under the flower head. Using a pair of pliers, fold back the middle sections of the marker from the centre of the flower to the edges of the petals.

5 Hold the two cut strips of the stem together so that the two halves of the bottom petal are joined. Using pliers, make a fold along the two outer lines of the stem. Wrap the stem around the cut section to hold the marker together.

MATERIALS AND EQUIPMENT YOU WILL NEED
TRACING PAPER • SOFT PENCIL • THIN CARD • SCISSORS • MARKER PEN • SHEET OF 38 GAUGE (0.004 IN) COPPER FOIL •
SHEET OF CHIPBOARD • BRADAWL • PLIERS

PEWTER-LOOK SHELF

ALUMINIUM FLASHING, TRADITIONALLY USED IN ROOFING, TAKES ON AN UNUSUAL, PITTED APPEARANCE THAT RESEMBLES PEWTER WHEN IT IS HAMMERED. IT CAN BE USED TO COVER SIMPLE SHAPES SUCH AS THIS SHELF AND IT IS VERY DIFFICULT TO GUESS WHAT THE ORIGINAL MATERIAL IS. PRACTISE YOUR HAMMERING TECHNIQUE ON AN OFF-CUT OF FLASHING FIRST TO ACHIEVE THE RIGHT TEXTURE, AND USE A BALL HAMMER TO MAKE SMOOTH, REGULAR INDENTATIONS. ALUMINIUM FLASHING MAY BE BOUGHT FROM ROOFING SUPPLIERS AND HARDWARE STORES.

1 Mark the two shelf pieces on MDF, using the template on page 94 as a guide. Cut them out with the handsaw. Draw a pencil line down the centre and mark two points for the drill holes. Mark corresponding points on the long edge of the stand. Drill holes at these points, then glue and screw the shelf and stand together.

2 Cut lengths of aluminium flashing roughly to size. Peel away the backing and stick them to the shelf front, trimming the rough edges on the side of the strips as you go.

3 Butt each new length of flashing very closely to the last, so that no MDF is visible beneath the covering.

4 When the front is covered, lay the shelf face down and carefully trim away the excess flashing using a craft knife.

5 Cut lengths of flashing to cover the back and sides of the shelf, and stick them in place.

6 Using a ball hammer, tap the surface of the flashing to make indentations close together. Vary the force with which you strike the flashing, so as to make an interesting and irregular pattern.

MATERIALS AND EQUIPMENT YOU WILL NEED

SHEET OF 18 MM (¾ IN) MDF (MEDIUM-DENSITY FIBREBOARD) • PENCIL • RULER • HANDSAW • DRILL • WOOD GLUE • 2 SCREWS • SCREWDRIVER • ALUMINIUM FLASHING • CRAFT KNIFE • BALL HAMMER

BARBECUE

OIL DRUMS ARE A GREAT SOURCE OF METAL AND ARE OFTEN SIMPLY DISCARDED, BUT THEY CAN BE GIVEN A NEW LEASE OF LIFE BY RECYCLING. THIS IS DONE IN MANY PARTS OF THE WORLD; IN HAITI, FOR EXAMPLE, DRUMS ARE HAMMERED FLAT AND USED TO MAKE DECORATIVE PAINTED CUT-OUTS. THEY ARE ALSO USED TO MAKE STEEL DRUMS, TOYS AND A WIDE VARIETY OF EVERYDAY HOUSEHOLD OBJECTS. HERE, AN OIL DRUM HAS BEEN INGENIOUSLY REUSED TO CREATE THIS BARBECUE. EVERY PART OF THE DRUM HAS BEEN USED AND A TIN CAN HAS BEEN TRANSFORMED INTO A CRAZILY ANGLED CHIMNEY STACK THAT GIVES IT THE APPEARANCE OF A SPACE ROCKET.

1 Wearing a work shirt and protective gloves, cut the oil drum in half using a hacksaw blade and tin shears. Draw two lines around the rim of the lower part of the drum, the first about 7 mm (¼ in) down and the second 2.5 cm (1 in) down. Place the grill on top of the drum and mark a point either side of where each bar of the grill touches the drum. As the bars of the grill run in only one direction, there will be a section on either side of the rim of the drum left unmarked. Using tin shears, cut down to the lower line from each of these points to make thin tabs.

2 Using pliers, bend the thin tabs outwards. Snip them shorter using tin shears, then bend them inwards and down to the inside of the drum.

3 Using pliers, grip the edge of each of the wider tabs where the upper line is drawn. Bend the edges over and squeeze them firmly to flatten them.

MATERIALS AND EQUIPMENT YOU WILL NEED

WORK SHIRT AND PROTECTIVE LEATHER GLOVES • OIL DRUM AND OIL DRUM SCRAPS • HACKSAW • TIN SHEARS • MARKER PEN • RULER • GRILL • PLIERS • FILE • LENGTH OF 2.5 CM (1 IN) DIAMETER DOWEL • WOODEN BLOCK • BRADAWL • ANNULAR RING NAILS • HAMMER • TRACING PAPER • SOFT PENCIL • THIN CARD • SCISSORS • DRILL • POP RIVETER AND RIVETS • TIN CAN

4 The grill should rest between the tabs. To make it sit securely you will need to cut the tabs near the unmarked side sections on a diagonal. Lay the grill on top of the drum and check that it sits properly on the drum.

5 To make the lid, draw a line around the other half of the drum, 1 cm (½ in) down from the cut edge. Cut equally spaced tabs around the rim as far as the line, using tin shears. Using pliers, bend over the tabs to the inside of the drum and flatten them.

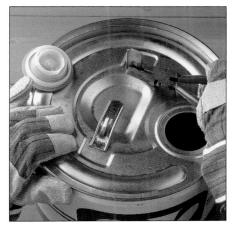

6 Remove the stopper from the top of the drum. Cut the handle in half using tin shears. Using pliers, bend both halves of the handle up at an angle of 90°. Cut the end of each half into a curve and file the edges of the halves smooth.

7 Cut a length of dowel to fit between the halves of the handle. Hold a wooden block against the side of each handle half and make a hole in each using a bradawl. File the rough edges around the holes smooth. Nail the handle halves to the dowel through the holes.

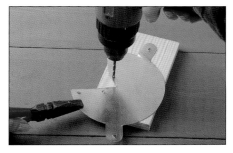

8 Draw the chimney roof pattern on to a spare piece of oil drum metal as shown here. Cut out the roof using tin shears and file the edges smooth. Place the roof on a block of wood and drill holes as shown. Hold the metal with a pair of pliers to stop it spinning round as you drill.

9 Gently curve the roof around so that the holes match and pop rivet the sides together.

10 Bend the roof tabs under. Place the tin on the tabs and mark where the edges of the tin touch them. Using pliers, bend the tabs back along the lines.

▶

11 For the chimney, open the other end of the tin can. Draw a line all the way around the tin to give the chimney a slanting base. Draw a second line parallel to the first and about 1 cm (½ in) above it. Draw four tabs at equal distances around the tin between the two lines. Cut around the upper line, leaving the tabs in place.

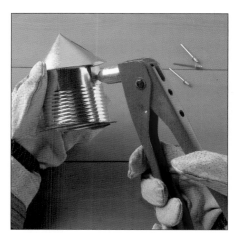

12 Place the roof on top of the chimney. Transfer the position of the holes in the tabs to the sides of the chimney. Drill holes in the side of the chimney and file away the rough edges. Pop rivet the roof to the chimney.

13 Stand the chimney on a block of wood and drill a hole in each tab. Place the chimney on the top of the lid. Transfer the position of the holes in the tabs to the lid. Drill the holes and file them smooth. Pop rivet the chimney to the lid.

14 Drill a hole every 5 cm (2 in) around the base of the barbecue to allow air to circulate when it is in use. File away the rough edges around the holes. When in use, the barbecue should never be left unattended.

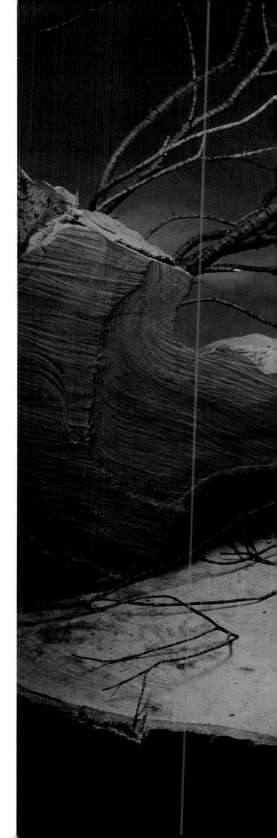

BIRD CHIMES

THIS WONDERFULLY ECCENTRIC FOUR-LEGGED BIRD FLOATS IN THE AIR AND PASSING BREEZES MOVE ITS LEGS, MAKING THEM CHIME. ITS BODY IS A TIN CAN AND THIN TIN PLATE HAS BEEN USED TO MAKE ITS WINGS, HEAD AND TAIL. THE BIRD IS PAINTED WITH ENAMEL PAINTS IN BRIGHT COLOURS THAT ACCENTUATE ITS CARTOON-LIKE BODY. PAINTS OF DIFFERENT COLOURS CAN BE APPLIED ON TOP OF EACH OTHER VERY SUCCESSFULLY, BUT THE FIRST COAT SHOULD BE ALLOWED TO DRY THOROUGHLY BEFORE THE SECOND IS ADDED TO PREVENT THE COLOURS RUNNING TOGETHER. USE HIGH-GAUGE TIN PLATE SO THAT IT IS EASY TO CURVE THE BIRD INTO SHAPE.

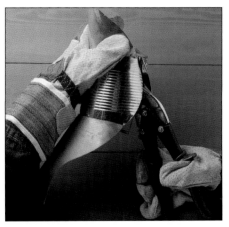

1 Using a tin opener, remove both ends of the tin can. Carefully file around the inside of each rim to remove all the rough edges. Trace the head, wing and tail templates from page 94, enlarging them as necessary and transfer them to thin card. Cut out the templates, lay them on the tin plate and draw around them. Wearing a work shirt and protective gloves, cut out all the shapes using tin shears. File around each piece to remove the rough edges.

2 Curve the head and tail sections around the tin can to shape them. Hold them in position on the tin using clothes pegs. Place the tin can on a soldering mat and, wearing a protective mask and goggles, apply flux and solder along the joins. Gently curve the two halves of the bird's head together and keep them in place with clothes pegs. Solder along the join. When the metal is cool, file around the beak to remove the sharp edges.

3 Using tin shears, cut a curve into the underside of the bird's body. Leave about 2 cm (¾ in) between the sides of the body at the narrowest point. File the edges smooth. Punch two holes on either side of the bird's body and one in the top using a hammer and nail. File away the rough edges around the holes. ▶

MATERIALS AND EQUIPMENT YOU WILL USE

TIN CAN • TIN OPENER • FILE • TRACING PAPER • SOFT PENCIL • THIN CARD • SCISSORS • THIN TIN PLATE •
WORK SHIRT AND PROTECTIVE LEATHER GLOVES • TIN SHEARS • CLOTHES PEGS • SOLDERING MAT • PROTECTIVE MASK AND GOGGLES • FLUX •
SOLDERING IRON AND SOLDER • HAMMER AND NAIL • MASKING TAPE • PLIERS • LENGTH OF 10 MM (½ IN) COPPER TUBING •
HACKSAW • G-CLAMP AND WOOD BLOCK • DRILL • FINE WIRE • SPLIT RING • METAL PRIMER • PAINTBRUSH • ENAMEL PAINTS

4 Attach the wings to the sides of the bird's body with strips of masking tape. Solder the wings to the body.

5 Using pliers, turn the edges of the wings over and squeeze them flat. Carefully file away any remaining rough edges. Do the same to finish the bird's tail.

6 To make the bird's legs, cut four 20 cm (8 in) lengths of copper tubing using a hacksaw. Cut each piece in half again and file away the rough edges.

7 Wrap strips of masking tape around the ends of the pieces of tubing. Firmly clamp each piece of tubing and drill a hole in each end. The masking tape will help to stop the drill bit from slipping. Join both halves of each leg together using short lengths of thin wire.

8 Cut four lengths of fine wire and use pliers to shape each piece into a foot. To join the feet to the bird's legs, push the ends of each foot into the holes in the end of the bird's legs and apply a dot of solder.

9 Pass a length of wire through one of the holes in the side of the bird's body. Attach a leg to the wire and twist the ends together to keep it in place. Attach the other three legs to the bird's body in the same way.

10 Using pliers, make a hook from fine wire and push it through the hole in the top of the bird's body. Attach a split ring to the hook to make a hanger. Apply one coat of metal primer to the bird, then a coat of bright yellow enamel paint. When the yellow paint has dried, add orange dots and the bird's features. Paint all its legs red and its feet blue.

TEMPLATES

EMBOSSED GREETINGS CARDS, PP24–25

CANDLE COLLARS, PP26–27

ROCKET CANDLESTICK, PP78–79

CHRISTMAS DECORATIONS, PP42–43

REINDEER, PP51–53

BATHROOM SHELF, PP55–57

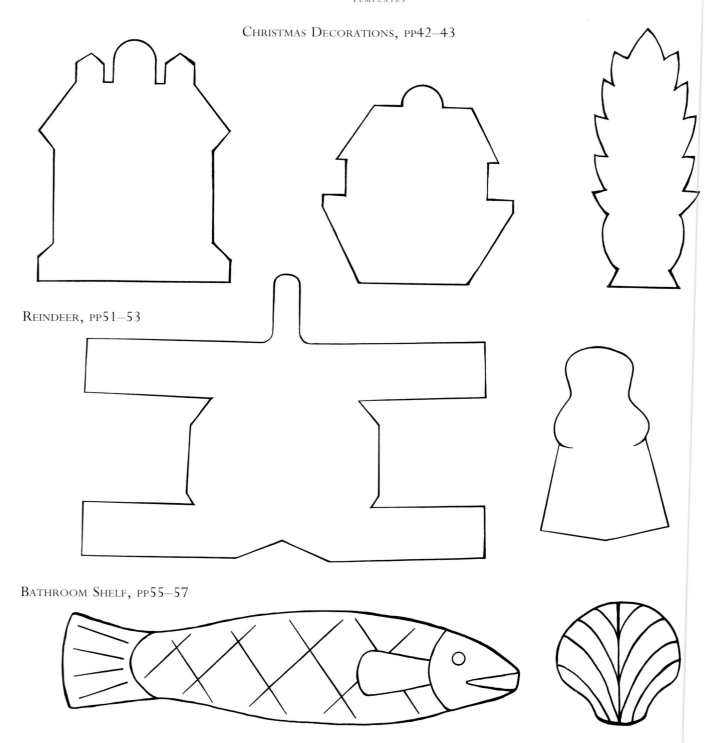

REGAL COAT RACK, PP66–68

LUNCH BOX, PP74–76

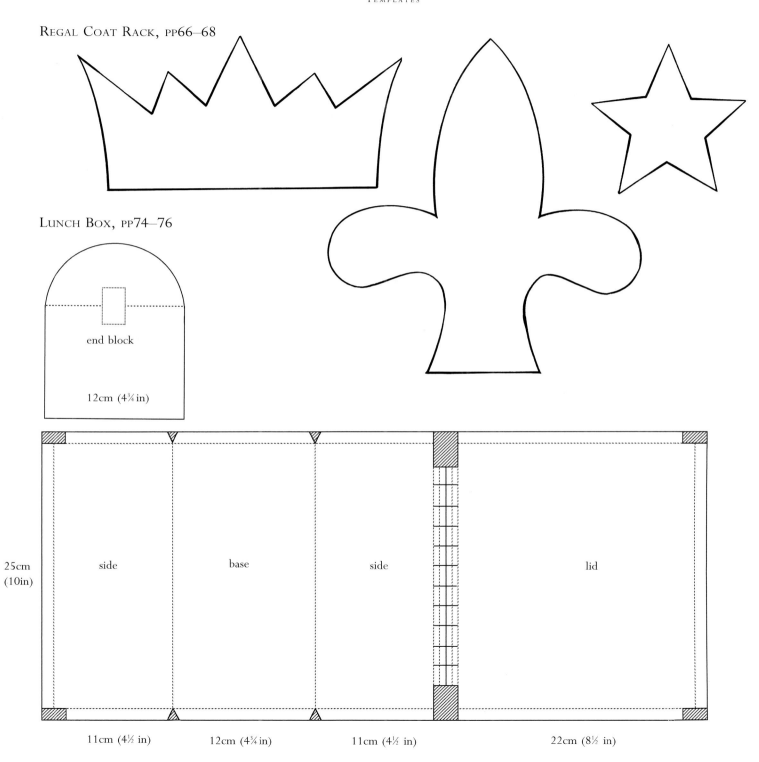

end block

12cm (4¾ in)

25cm
(10in)

side

base

side

lid

11cm (4½ in) 12cm (4¾ in) 11cm (4½ in) 22cm (8½ in)

BIRD CHIMES, PP88–90

PLANT MARKER, PP80–81

PEWTER-LOOK SHELF, PP82–83

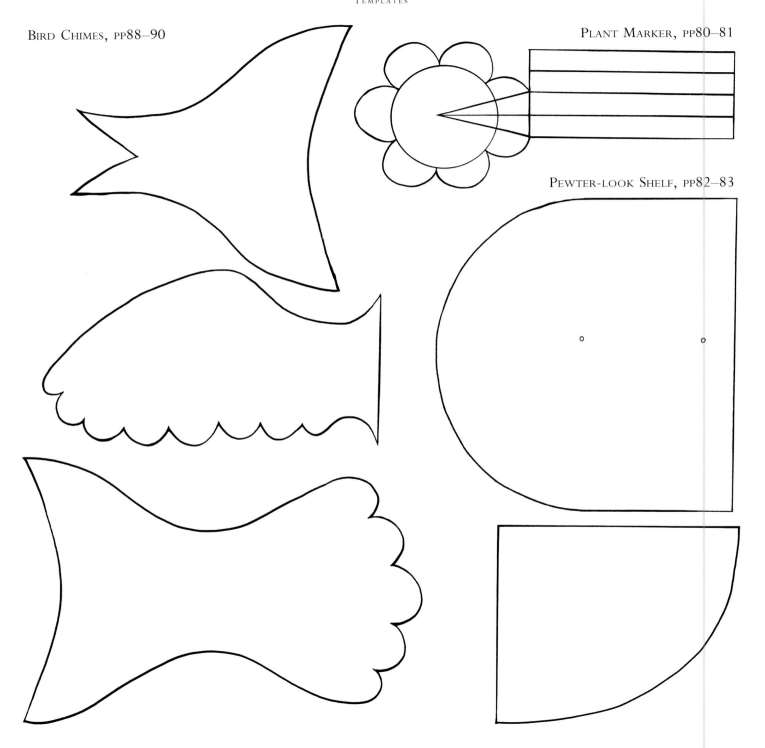

SUPPLIERS

Most of the equipment used in this book, such as solder, solder guns and flux, can be obtained from good hardware shops. Many of the projects are made out of recycled tin, and the metal foils that are used in others can be bought in large craft shops. A few of the projects require more specialist materials, and listed below are suppliers who sell these items.

Australia

Tinplate Distribution P/L
Angas Street
Meadowbank
NSW 2114
Tel: 02 808 1522

Suppliers of tin plate

NCI Diversified Products P/L
Separation Street
Northcote
Victoria 3070
Tel: 03 9489 0666

Suppliers of tin plate

Mitre
(10 stores nationally – check directory for local stockist)

Suppliers of tin snips and general hardware goods. Some stores carry sheets of tin

Handwork Supplies P/L
Commercial Road
South Yarra
Victoria 3141
Tel: 03 9820 8399

Stockists of aluminium, gold and brass shim. Run workshops in metalcraft

Arts Papers-Gemrocks P/L
Springvale Road
Nunawading
Victoria 3131
Tel: 03 9877 5779

Stocks most metal working tools, including pliers and tin snips

McEwans
Bourke Street
Melbourne
Victoria 3000
Tel: 03 9607 0777

General hardware

Home Hardware and Thrifty Link Hardware
Lower Dandenong Road
Braeside
Victoria 3195
Tel: 03 9607 0777

Stockists of tin snips, pliers and scribers

Canada

Abbey Arts & Crafts
Hastings Street
Burnaby, B.C.
Tel: 604 299 5201

Suppliers of metal foils, and general materials and equipment

Dundee Hobby Craft
1518–6551 No 3 Road
Richmond, B.C.
Tel: 604 278 5713

Suppliers of metal foils, and general materials and equipment

Fun Craft City Ltd
13890–104 Avenue
Surrey, B.C.
Tel: 604 583 3262

Suppliers of metal foils, and general materials and equipment

Lee Valley
S.W. Marine Drive
Vancouver, B.C.
Tel: 604 261 2262

General equipment

Lee Valley
Steeles Avenue W. Westin
Toronto, Ontario
Tel: 416 746 0850

General equipment

United Kingdom

Clay Brothers
Metal Suppliers
The Green
High Street
Ealing
London W5 5DA
Tel: 0181 567 2215

Suppliers of non-ferrous metals such as tin plate. Also suppliers of all sorts of nuts, bolts, screws and tools, such as tin snips. Shop and mail-order supply

J Smith & Sons
Tottenham Road
Islington
London N1 4BZ
Tel: 0171 253 1277

Suppliers of metal and metal foil

Alec Tiranti
Warren Street
London W1 5DG
Tel: 0171 636 8565

Sculptor's supplies – stock shim and metal foils

Buck and Ryan
Tottenham Court Road
London W1V ODY
Tel: 0171 636 7475

Stocks a wide range of tools including tin snips, shears and leather gloves

ACKNOWLEDGEMENTS

The publishers and author would like to thank all the people who helped compile this book, particularly the contributors who made the projects: Penny Boylan, page 24; Deborah Schneebeli Morrell, page 26 and 42; Evelyn Bennett, page 38, 47, 53, 60, 72 and 89; Mary Maguire, page 64, and Andrew Gilmore, page 74, 78, 80, 82, 84. They would also like to thank the following shops and collections for lending further tinware items for photography: Young & D Ltd, Beckhaven House, 9 Gilbert Road, London SE11 5AA (Tel: 0171 820 9403) for the collection of Greek tinware, page 6–7; the Tony Hayward Collection for the tin cars, page 8, and the projector, page 15; Applachia – the Folk Art Shop, 14A St George Street, St Albans, Herts (Tel: 01727 836796) for the cookie cutters on page 9, and the Kasbah, 8 Southampton Street, London WC2E 7HA (Tel: 0171 240 3538) for the lanterns on page 9.

The following artists would be pleased to accept commissions for tinwork: Lucy Casson, 39 Jeffreys Road, London SW4 6QU; Val Hunt, 14 Baginton Road, Coventry CV3 6JW; Andy Hazell, Grosvenor Mill, Wincolmelee, Hull HU2 8AH; Joanne Tinker, 13 Fern Terrace, Stanningley, Leeds LS28 6JA; Michael Marriot, 6 Weaver House, Pedley Street, London E1 5ES; Julia Foster, c/o Publisher; Adrian Taylor, Studio 42, Great Western Studios, Great Western Road, London W9 3NY, and Nick Shinnie, c/o Publisher.

AUTHOR'S ACKNOWLEDGEMENTS

The author would like to thank Clare Nicholson for all her organization and enthusiasm; Joanna Lorenz; Peter Williams for his wonderful photography; Neil Hadfield for his woodworking skills, and all the contributors.

INDEX